HERE ON EARTH

THE LANDSCAPE IN NEW ZEALAND LITERATURE

HERE ON EARTH

THE LANDSCAPE IN NEW ZEALAND LITERATURE

INTRODUCTION BY DAVID EGGLETON

PHOTOGRAPHS BY CRAIG POTTON

CRAIG
POTTON
PUBLISHING

Photographs: Craig Potton (except where otherwise credited)
Introduction: David Eggleton
Text Selection: David Eggleton, Craig Potton and Robbie Burton
Production: Tina Delceg, Arnott Potter and Robbie Burton
Printing: Astra Print Ltd, Wellington

Published by Craig Potton Publishing, Box 555, Nelson, New Zealand
©1999 Craig Potton Publishing
Copyright in individual pieces of writing remains vested in the authors.

ISBN 0 908802 52 8

CONTENTS

DAVID EGGLETON *Introduction* — 6

C K STEAD *After the Wedding* — 24

JAMES K BAXTER *High Country Weather* — 28

JAMES K BAXTER *Poem in the Matukituki Valley* — 30

JAMES K BAXTER *At the Fox Glacier Hotel* — 32

KATHERINE MANSFIELD from *At the Bay* — 34

KAPKA KASSABOVA from *Reconnaissance* — 37

OWEN MARSHALL *There Is A Place...* — 40

ELIZABETH KNOX *When We Stopped* — 42

BASIL DOWLING *Canterbury* — 44

RUTH DALLAS *In Central Otago* — 46

JOHN MULGAN from *Man Alone* — 48

JOHN A LEE from *Delinquent Days* — 52

H GUTHRIE-SMITH from *Tutira: The Story of a New Zealand Sheep Station* — 55

FIONA FARRELL from *A Story About Skinny Louie* — 58

HONE TUWHARE *Kaka Point* — 60

HONE TUWHARE *The old place* — 62

RONALD HUGH MORRIESON from *Came a Hot Friday* — 64

FRANK SARGESON from *Once Is Enough* — 66

DENIS GLOVER *Wellington Harbour – Dead Calm* — 70

JOHN NEWTON *Opening The Book* — 72

SAMUEL BUTLER from *Erewhon* — 74

MAURICE SHADBOLT from *A Touch Of Clay* — 77

A R D FAIRBURN *The Estuary* — 80

IAN WEDDE from *Symmes Hole* — 82

IAN WEDDE from *Dick Seddon's Great Dive* — 84

PATRICIA GRACE from *Waiariki* — 88

ALLEN CURNOW *You Will Know When You Get There* — 90

ALISTAIR TE ARIKI CAMPBELL *Sanctuary Of Spirits* — 92

CHARLES BRASCH from *Indirections* — 94

AAT VERVOORN from *Beyond the Snowline* — 97

SAM HUNT *A White Gentian* — 100

WITI IHIMAERA from *Tangi* — 102

JANET FRAME from *Living in the Maniototo* — 107

KIRSTY GUNN from *Rain* — 110

GEOFF PARK from *Nga Uruora – The Groves of Life* — 112

CHRIS ORSMAN *Ornamental Gorse* — 116

LAURIS EDMOND *September* — 118

MAURICE GEE from *Plumb* — 120

BRUCE MASON from *End of the Golden Weather* — 122

KERI HULME from *Slipping Away from the Gaze of the Past* — 124

M K JOSEPH *Distilled Water* — 130

BRIAN TURNER *Visiting Kai Kai Beach* — 132

CHARLIE DOUGLAS from *Mr Explorer Douglas* — 134

INTRODUCTION

David Eggleton

Every landscape is a museum of extracts, an anthology of fragments, an album of glimpses. Feelings about places haunt us and inspire us. We seek clues in the landscape for answers to the riddle, the secret of where we are, who we are, here on earth. Landscapes are skeins of connections and recollections, of inklings and murmurs. There is some deep, personal distillation of concept and emotion in our favourite landscapes, those places to which we often return, even if only in memory.

Manawhenua is that sense of belonging that connects people and land. The landscape of Aotearoa New Zealand is our cultural centre of gravity, our leading literary theme, our dominant metaphor. We inscribe it with our hopes and dreams; the land is our waka, our location beacon, a site of layered history. Landscape is a state of mind: the environment that determines the character of a people; it is a map of our assumptions, desires, projections – the tricky jigsaw of coastline, the long, thin, windswept shape of islands, the totemic mountains, the 'sharp and sudden contrasts'.

To describe New Zealand is to invent it. 'The characteristic fauna of the North Island are chthonic gods', glimpsed visiting historian Arnold Toynbee. 'At Rotorua their breath rises in clouds of steam from the bush and their mouths gape to spit out boiling sulphurous spume.' Katherine Mansfield, in her short story 'The Woman at the Store', also stares perceptively: 'There is no twilight in our New Zealand days but a curious half-hour when everything appears grotesque – it frightens – as though the savage spirit of the country walked abroad and

sneered at what it saw'. James K Baxter distilled the place where he lived into poetry: 'For us the land is matrix and destroyer' – and in another poem he intoned, as though something or someone had whispered it in his ear: 'This is a country made for angels, not for men'. Charles Brasch, equally vatic, equally ecstatic, also sensed the presence of the angelic orders: 'The thousand mountains shining/ Lifting their rock and snow/ Into upper air, ocean of light'. Keri Hulme however didn't sense angels – she saw those angry chthonic gods: 'I watch the waves wage their long war/ against the land, the land her long resistance'. Everywhere conflict, turmoil, tension, turbulence.

'New Zealand' is a site of competing versions, a site of struggle: aesthetic consideration clashes with commercial consideration; conservation clashes with exploitation; methods of ownership are disputed – individual pitted against communal, communal pitted against corporate, corporate pitted against state; Maori negotiates with Pakeha; national versus multinational; heritage versus progress; meanwhile climate, geology, topography exert their own pressures in the Shaky Isles – 'this far-pitched perilous hostile place/ this solitary hard-assaulted spot', as R A K Mason hymned it in 1924. Meaning, use and purpose get debated, communities of interest are formed, voices are raised. The landscape is always being looked at in a new light, with fresh eyes. It goes on being transformed – sometimes, as research scientist and writer Geoff Park has noted, it returns to what it was, germinating out of the last traces of the 'original land' into lush pockets of eco-logical recovery. As he says, whether saved by design, by Maori protest, or by the accident of being forgotten about: 'Nature now is more novelty than nuisance'.

Writers name places into existence, offering ways of seeing, ways of understanding, presenting responses to various land-scapes with various microclimates. 'Landscape', as historian Simon Schama observes in *Landscape and Memory* is a 'text on which generations write their recurring obsessions'. Maori living here evolved their own mythology over hundreds of years, weaving an organic tracery of stories to explain where they were to themselves. So Maoritanga, then, contains a magical, folkloric landscape, the logical outcome of voyage myths, the tribal product of bards and orators. When Captain James Cook sailed up the coast to make landfall in the late eighteenth century, he was propelled philosophically by the ideas of the European Enlightenment, and commercially by British Imperial expansionist policies. He was the symbolic prime mover in a new world order of noble savages, pastoral promises and humanist hopes. After him came the deluge and the growth of the New Zealand mind: a land, a landscape, a nation. Cook's glowing reports back in London on the possi-bilities of 'settlement' fired up prospective colonists. Cook helped launch a new mythology – taken up enthusiastically by arch-colonist Edward Gibbon Wakefield – of an English pasto-ral Arcadia which might one day become a Utopia in the South Pacific.

When the first British settlers began arriving, however, they saw not a new England but an alien landscape from which they would have to wrestle meaning. This landscape had its own mysterious oppressive beauty to come to terms with – the ironsand beach, the heavy surf, the flax swamp, the fold after fold of dark hills, the cloud veiling the steep face of a moun-tain. For them this place was, as poet Basil Dowling wrote a hundred years later, 'anonymous though named'.

In his novel *Symmes Hole* (1986), with its specific density of details and its roughcast sensuality, Ian Wedde provides an early nineteenth century South Pacific pastoral, featuring whalers, sealers, explorers, and local Maori tribes all rubbing along together in a kind of ersatz-Polynesian parody of the schemes Wakefield was busy organising. *Symmes Hole* is partly an account of James Heberley's search for a home in the New Zealand of the 1830s, when it still seemed possible for Maori and European to co-exist without wholesale destruction of the indigenous way of life. In the margin between Western civilisa-tion and Pacific culture, exotic hybrids might flower in com-munities which anticipate sixties hippie communal idealism, or even the latter-day Polynesian pastoral of Witi Ihimaera and Patricia Grace. It was glad, confident morning in New Zealand, and in that early period of cross-cultural anarchy a different kind of Utopia to Wakefield's did indeed seem possible:

Where his course took him inshore he'd hear the big pigeons and the tuis thrashing about in the branches of the early berry trees. The tui'd be watering up his song, getting the trickle of it right. And he'd hear the pipping of warblers, and big hoarse blackback gulls checking the dory. The peaceful morning would move in on his senses, he'd hear how the calm was a net of sounds … and (smell) the low-water reek of seaweeds and washed-up bush wrack – tart flavours that spread through his nostrils jaded from the greasy beach, like a drink of spring-water amber with leafmould.

Wedde's late twentieth century version of the romantic sublime – James Heberley's apotheosis as a natural man à la Jean-Jacques Rousseau, dwelling amongst Maori, living off the land, becoming at one with himself and place – is based on the historical record. In the early nineteenth century New Zealand was crawling with adventurers and freebooters, traders and explorers, caught up in the notion of New Zealand as a untamed wilderness – here was romanticism sanctified by the transcendent verities of earth and sky. In 1757 Edmund Burke had published his profoundly influential *On the Sublime and Beautiful*, a treatise which helped legitimise the whole Romantic movement – the idea of the primacy of the self at the centre of things and of awe for its own sake as response to the natural world. Burke defined the sublime 'as productive of the strongest emotion of which the mind is capable of feeling'. Burke created a philosophic space for mountains and scenery. If the sublime was characterised by magnificence and greatness, then New Zealand fitted right in. This new land, with its beautiful mountains and treacherous rivers, was a preordained site of heroic action.

In *Yesterdays in Maoriland: New Zealand in the 1880s* Andreas Reischek describes a storm he experienced high up in southern Fiordland:

… one moment enveloped in thick darkness, the next dazzled by flashes of lightning … The Sounds below, the naked peaks above, and the realm of bush between were lit up in marvellous detail. I could see an enormous waterspout dancing with insane speed … This storm was … sublime.

For Reischek the landscape is epic primal theatre. This high country, as illuminated by flashes of lightning is a maelstrom, a vortex, reverberating with the awesome energy of the heavens. He confirms Burke's thesis that wild landscapes 'are capable of producing delight, not pleasure but a sort of delightful horror, a sort of tranquillity tinged with terror'. Here is the rapture of a new country being written into existence.

Expeditions into the wilderness, roughing it through wild New Zealand, led explorers to marvel over the intense clarity of the sky, especially in mountainous country where the air was as translucent as crystal. William Pember Reeves in *The Long White Cloud* (1898), his history of New Zealand, describes going out in the very early mornings of still midsummer days:

Then, before the air is heated or troubled or tainted, but when night seems to have cooled and purged from it all impurity, far off ridges and summits stand out clean, sharp and vivid … On such a morning from a hill looking northward over league after league of rolling virgin forest I have seen the great volcano Mount Ruapehu rear up his 9000 feet, seeming a solitary mass, the upper part distinctly seen, blue and snow-capped, the lower bathed and half-lost in a pearl-coloured haze.

Other writers attempting the sublime were less successful. Poet and premier of New Zealand Alfred Domett produced a labyrinthian poem, called 'Ranolf and Amohia: A South-Sea day-dream' (1872), which is stocked with jumble-sale junk from a warehouse of romantic period-piece imagery.

The solitary outcast of romantic iconography, though, is a significant figure in the New Zealand landscape. Charlie Douglas, Mr Explorer Douglas, was a real-life character, one of the most persistent of explorers, who spent four decades surveying and mapping South Westland. Born in Edinburgh in 1840, he migrated to Otago in 1862 and then headed to the West Coast. Hardy and frugal, he lived off the land, and was an attentive observer. His diaries are a mine of practical information, presented in a wry, often sardonic, self-deprecating style. Charlie Douglas was the man who went bush and stayed there.

The explorer-hero myth was partly a product of the imperial narrative. The explorer was the forerunner of a conquering army, a warning of colonial dispossession, of Eurocentric appropriation. The search for the picturesque concealed a drive for power – expressed literally soon enough by steam power engines and turbines, and later by dams and hydroelectric stations. But parallel with this British Imperial narrative, which began emerging almost immediately after the signing of the Treaty of Waitangi in 1840, there was the parallel narrative of the marginalised Byronic hero. The 'bush' is the last refuge of the natural, self-reliant man, and of the outlaw, in the novels of William Satchell and Jane Mander and later in *Man Alone* (1939), by John Mulgan. The tradition continued with Barry Crump's yarns about misfit blokes in the bush in his string of novels. Another of these folk heroes is Mackenzie the sheep rustler in James McNeish's eponymous novel, where Mackenzie is celebrated as a romantic visionary, an ecstatic who responds to the rhythms of the Antipodean seasons and to the awesome landscape of the Canterbury high country by becoming a ragged-trousered prophet who intends to lead his people – the squatters – to this promised land: 'He never marched the Sabbath. He would find a stream and read aloud from the Book of Psalms; for the land in its variety seemed to him not unlike a Psalm of David'.

But in the end the pristine land Mackenzie discovered is made over:

The ugliness was almost breathtaking: a scatter of fenced farms, of dirty sheds, of matted ditches and manic gorse, of higgledy-piggledy wagons and engines and railway lumber … the new men spoke in a voice of fatigued clarity and declared the original landscape to be at last unrecognisable.

Mackenzie, quester after a religious vision of the land, a product of mythic history, remains in McNeish's version, the unacknowledged sage, an alternative to the great bearded sages of the colonial administration in Christchurch and Wellington.

Now, where explorers once probed the alpine fastnesses, slowly climbing the lower slopes of formidable crags, pausing to sketch, map or note-take, or sometimes just to get their bearings, helicopters, light aircraft and passenger jets wing their way overhead and four-wheel drive vehicles and late-model cars hurry by along sealed roads. From today's viewpoint the first settlers were just out to tame and subdue an obstreperous landscape by brute force, but the settlers saw themselves as having a higher purpose. They engaged with the landscape in order to draw from it consolatory meanings and moral precepts; we are their inheritors, though sometimes their Victorian virtues may become our vices and their vices our virtues. After the elation of the sublime, there was Christianity. For the missionaries any sense of nature's terrifying strangeness had to be denied, excluded, shut down, lest the land cast a spell.

Maori place-names are often metaphoric, that is they summon up, or at least refer to the mauri: the indwelling spirit of place. In these names, animism, pantheism and anthropomorphism – a whole panoply of the pagan – are active concepts. The waves of British migrants who arrived in orderly fashion in New Zealand in the early years of settlement, brought here mainly by the Wakefield-linked organisations – the New Zealand Company, the Canterbury Association, the Otago Association – carried not only their English town names, and everything they implied, with them (Wellington, New Plymouth, Nelson, Christchurch) but also their religion: their Christian factions. They were believers in Divine plans, they were members of God's elect, guided and protected by Providence. They were coming to a land of darkness inhabited by heathen. They were, as Edward Gibbon Wakefield declared in his manifesto *The British Colonisation of New Zealand*: 'taking God and civilisation to the furtherest ends of the earth'. Missionaries such as the Reverend Richard Taylor confirmed the theological significance of place: the brooding landscapes of the interior were 'blasted by sin'. The European had a duty both to convert the Maori to Christianity and to convert the landscape to Christian principles. The wilderness represented evil and ignorance.

Wakefield's plans for colonising the 'waste lands' of New Zealand, leaving aside the watercolour tints of the 'picturesque' mountains, as he fondly envisaged them, led him to write a glowing picture of agricultural and pastoral opportunities in a land he'd never seen. He painted a picture of Utopian bliss and bountiful harvests based on a dream of a Romantic pre-industrial England. Settlers who bought into this line of propaganda had a rude shock waiting for them. Historian James Belich in *Making Peoples* (1996) quotes an early settler's reaction in a letter home to England in 1840: New Zealand was 'a gloomy country, without flowers, or fruits, or birds, or insects. I cannot but fancy it accursed'. Another disgruntled settler wrote in 1842: 'one of the wildest places you can imagine, very mountainous, everywhere so thickly wooded that you cannot walk without a path being cut'.

The land was an arena, the centre of a dialectic. The clash was between the natural wilderness and the landscape of cultivation the settlers sought. The bush as a pagan place of beginnings, the dark forest of origin, was rejected – the endless acres of indigenous trees were to be sacrificed to the concept of progress. Pakeha worked hard and fast in a blind fervour to farm and replicate the European ideal. Yet, despite these efforts the countryside remained haunting, mysterious. (In the 1820s Dumont D'Urville described the land as 'solemn, almost sinister'. The visiting British novelist J B Priestley used the same description in the 1970s: the landscape was 'sinister, strangely menacing'.) The forest was oppressive and land was something to be won from the enemy, nature. The settlers, as

Monte Holcroft later wrote were engaged in a 'struggle against the forest'. The natural forest cover of the plains country, 'the forest shadow of another New Zealand' as Geoff Park calls it, was systematically eradicated. 'Rationalised landscapes of square paddocks and dead straight roads' were created by the surveyor's theodolite. The forest was cut and burnt and exotic flora and fauna were released.

The new Victorian order was paternalistic and militaristic, carving up tracts of virgin wilderness – a feminine landscape – there to be conquered, made obedient. The writer Samuel Butler came to New Zealand in 1860 as part of the land rush in Canterbury organised by Wakefield. He wrote *Erewhon* (1872), a novel about a backwards Utopia, partly as a riposte to Wakefield's misleading idealism and to the prevailing provincial complacency he encountered. Yet he also held some of those attitudes himself. In *Erewhon* the sublime landscape begins merging with the practical: the luminous prose-painting of landscape in the first part of the book gives way to an account of a mechanistic society. New Zealand had to be normalised by destroying the alien and indigenous and substituting the social and material forms of the metropolitan homeland of England, a process encouraged and accelerated by New Zealand's government. As Butler pointed out in *A First Year in Canterbury Settlement* (1863): 'A mountain here is only beautiful if it has good grass on it, if it is good for sheep'. Yet this claim is undercut, challenged even, by other contemporary writers. The balladeer David McKee Wright celebrated simple delight in landscape:

There's pleasure working in the sun and frost and wind and rain,
There's glory on the mountain top and on the shining plain,
There's fragrance in the spear-grass fire, there's music in the creek…

And Butler's own first sight of Mount Cook is in the true spirit of the sublime: 'I was struck almost breathless by the wonderful mountain that burst upon my sight. The effect was startling. It rose towering in a massy parallelogram disclosed from top to bottom in the cloudless sky, far above all others'.

Meanwhile the battle to place each new settler at the end of a mud road went on. John A Lee described the settler's axe as 'cutting a thousand years of timber to make a home'. The climax of exploration, of naming and claiming, of charting and surveying, was the hacking of farms out of the bush. Hacking and burning: 'flame and blade, fire and axe' as poet Ursula Bethell wrote. Settlers transformed alien space into a home place by firing grassland and forest, draining swamps and sowing imported grasses. Landscape as villain, to be fired where it stood, resulted in huge burn-offs, uncontrollable bush fires of apocalyptic proportions – 34 houses burnt down in Stratford, 10,000 sheep incinerated on one station alone in Canterbury.

Jessie Mackay's poem 'Spring Fires', inspired by the spring burn-off of tussock on the Canterbury Plains is an ardent hymn to the fertility of the moon, in which she sings of the 'slow running' fire as 'a pure red moth … winging to the snow' and which rises to a fever pitch of ecstasy: 'we know it and we know it, but we love the moon of fire'. The flavour of the colonial soil, though, is that of ashes. Blanche Baughan in 1908 in the poem 'A Bush Section' described how after a fire 'the tumultuous landscape/ Is struck and prickled, and spiked with the standing black and grey splinters'. The funeral pyre of the primeval was built out of the children of Tane, god of the forest.

Samuel Butler, in the middle of the Victorians' victorious century, represented the pragmatic, triumphant attitude of the colonist when he wrote positively: 'The fire dries up many swamps – at least many disappear after the country has been once or twice burnt; the water moves more freely, unimpeded by the tangled and decaying vegetation and the sun gets freer access to the ground'. By contrast for William Pember Reeves, writing fifteen years later, the destruction of the swamps verged on vandalism:

Small streams ran out of the swamp … and disappeared in the shingle of the beach. When not disturbed with draining work, their water was sweet and clear. The swamps had been covered with tall flax, toetoe, rushes and small bushes, green and beautiful in the sunlight, but as the drains did their work, the peat sank, cracked and dried, the surface was systematically burnt and became stretches of black hideous ashes and mud, poached up by the hoofs of cattle.

A vanished ecosystem, a vanished frieze: erosion, flooding, destabilisation – we've created 'a landscape of warnings' according to Geoff Park. Yet there is also the popular chocolate box-lid sentiment as lyricised by Alan Mulgan in 1958, still echoing the earliest colonial policy: 'English trees and crops have added greatly to the beauty and graciousness of our landscape. Think of the chequer-board of cultivation on the Canterbury Plains, once a waste of tussock and scrub; Lombardy poplars among South Island mountains, in autumn towers of gold against distant snow'.

By the 1890s 'The Land with all Wood and Waters' that Captain Cook had espied had been dramatically altered. But now that the ancient forests of the lowlands had been largely eradicated by the scorched earth policies of successive governments, the nation became preservation-conscious. The 1892 Land Act and the Scenery Preservation Act of 1903 established a series of national parks and wildlife sanctuaries, as well as recognising Maori sacred places. The thick green twilight, the gloomy green night of New Zealand's forest interiors, had been rolled back. The green citadel had been stormed and subdued.

'It's not what the landscape says/ but the way that it's said', avers C K Stead in his poem 'After the Wedding' (1988). By the end of the nineteenth century the common memory of place, the New Zealand built up out of explorer and pioneer narratives, had begun to be refreshed by a multitude of other accounts – other myths, motifs, many-angled truths. The 'inland eye', as critic E H McCormick termed it, the eye of the settler's descendant, began to contemplate the landscape around about with a certain intimacy and affection, as delicately as a gecko sipping nectar from pohutukawa blossom. The sublime was replaced by the scenic. Blanche Baughan's *Studies in New Zealand Scenery* (1916) is a series of vignettes. In one she journeys by boat up the Wanganui River to discover 'All is one fairyland of green … the spell of the river has fallen upon us'. The tree fern is 'a princeling of the forest … its great green drooping coronet keeping the sky from us … (the ferns) massed together … look like encampments of fairy pavilions'. As the boat glides along her eye is drawn again and again to 'some secret grotto of greenness'. Visiting Milford Sound, Baughan wrote of 'the simple vision of one perfect, far-off ivory peak'.

Finding delicate beauty in details of scenery with the occasional luminous poetic image, Baughan echoes (in a landscape full of echoes) both Lady Barker of forty years earlier: 'There was no tint of colour except green when once we passed the red-fringed curtain of rata-branches, only the white and shining fairy beach and the gleaming threads of water' – and the tourist pastiche of forty years later, which photographs and writes euphemistically about New Zealand as one continuous beauty spot.

Robin Hyde, in the 1930s, wrote more robustly, offering the sensation that the land underfoot is alive:

The land was living, like the sea. A land's always alive while it can grow hair, and this place sent up scrub and trees, gorse and bracken, long grasses that wear slippery in summer when feet run over them. Beyond Thorndon, black and slatternly, the city was guarded by the full monster strength of a range lying with its head on its blunt paws. It was quick soil, ready. The whole earth was filled with the potency of moving again if it liked, of feeling all contacts strongly through its veins and marrow. The children who ran across it were moving inside its movement, like kites on a string controlled by its big will.

At round the same time further south, from her home on the Cashmere Hills looking out towards the Southern Alps, poet Ursula Bethell was writing this: 'I witnessed/ Resting on a garden bench and looking westward/ Sublime splendours/ … Wild indigo and magenta rainstorms invested the dark recesses of the mountain ranges./ Clouds overhead burst into cornelian flames … then was revealed … a young … slender … moon'. Drawing on Anglican devotional writing – the hymnal, the prayerbook, the Scriptures, 'very earnestly digging', cultivating her garden, Bethell produced gorgeous incantations about landscape which dripped with symbolism. Nature was celebrated, in the manner of Gerard Manley Hopkins, as God's handiwork: mountains were the transcendental fulcrum between earth and air. This was the sublime as sublimated erotic feeling – the landscape was charged with a baroque tension: 'Bronze tussocked terraces before precipitous/ Great purple alps, loose glacier-shed/ Fierce-laughing streams in circuitous riverbed'.

'Reading the landscape', Geoff Park tells us in *Nga Uruora* –

The Groves of Life (1995), a modern-day exploration of aspects of New Zealand's natural environment, 'you can only catch some of the infinite detail. The rest is washed away beyond memory and possession'. The New Zealand environment is all details: the heart of the country may as equally be found in out-of-the-way places as in the muddy centre. The relatively sparse population causes Cilla McQueen to imagine in her poem 'Living Here' that 'this place is just one big city', with its 'suburbs strung out in a long line' north to south, between ocean horizon and hill range monoliths. You still don't have to go far from your front door or back door to swallow nature whole, in great gulps of illumination. James K Baxter has named the key themes which occur again and again in this nation's poetry: they are the sea, the island, the beach, the bush, the mountain; our history is in the metaphysical richness of our landscape. Denis Glover wrote in 'Arawata Bill' (1953):

In the dominion of the thorn
The delicate cloud is born,
And golden nuggets bloom
in the womb of the storm

Frost-bright stars, the 'cool noiseless forests', mountains glistening white against a dazzling blue sky, the snow-fed river torrents of spring, the earth itself smelling moist; the rainforest odour, as William Pember Reeves wrote, of 'blended resin, sappy wood, damp leaves, and brown tinder (which) hangs in the air'. Lady Barker asserted: 'In no other part of the world does Nature so thoroughly understand how to make a fine day as in New Zealand'. And the land is volatile – a place of eruptions, floods, earthquakes.

In *My Simple Life in New Zealand* (1908) Adela B Stewart describes her brush with the 1886 eruption of Mount Tarawera ('this was *not* rain, but dust and ashes quietly falling in the dim twilight at noon'). Ruth Park, in her childhood memoir *A Fence Around the Cuckoo* (1992), recalls the effect of the 1931 Napier earthquake on the Coromandel coast:

On a still hot morning, February 3, an extraordinary phenomenon occurred. The tide went out and didn't come back in … It quietly withdrew. (We) were fooling around in the shallows in the dinghy at the time, and I felt this withdrawal abruptly, as though the water had been yanked away from underneath. We bumped and dragged on the stony bottom … The water went east … there was no fuss of waves, no sound except gentle lapping. It went out so far we could no longer see it; there was a ruffling line of steely glitter in the middle of the Gulf, and that was that.

The tide stayed out all day. Sometime in the night there was movement without form, as though a great body stretched itself in the darkness, and the sea returned with a sigh and a rattle of stones …

New Zealand is where, as a poem by Kapka Kassabova points out, 'all roads lead to the sea'. In 'Landfall in Unknown Seas', written to commemorate the 300th anniversary of the discovery of New Zealand by Abel Tasman, Allen Curnow imagines Tasman's first sight of 'the seascape/ Crammed with coast, surprising/ As new lands will, the sailor …'. Ian Wedde, in his long poem 'Pathway to the Sea' (a literal translation of the Maori placename Aramoana), offers a worm's eye view of a backyard trench being dug towards the sea. Robin Hyde goes to the beach and inhales the 'smell of the sun-soaked, salt-white wood'. Out there, she notes, is 'the green Pacific, with her waiting eyes'. Poet Eileen Duggan looks above the ocean to the bright sky: 'The great Pacific salt so steeps our air/ That noon-tide burns it to a driftwood blue'.

This is a country where earth, sea and sky interpenetrate.

Travelling through the Marlborough Sounds in 1872, novelist Anthony Trollope notes 'the headlands and broken bays with the rough steep mountains coming sheer down into the blue waters'. In the Marlborough Sounds nearly a hundred years later, Denis Glover muses: 'There is always water./ Every track, half-road or hilltop/ Throws a view of the labyrinthine/ Seeping and effortless sea …'.

Allen Curnow, in the great outdoors, elects to prowl the wild West Coast of Auckland of the 1990s, all crashing waves and undertow, where colour 'ricochets' and where 'the helicopter/ clapper-clawed the sea' – this marine din hinting at a great city nearby. 'Auckland, the Gulf, sailing, sunburn, beaches where you are remote enough not to have to worry about putting on bathing things', wrote James Bertram in a letter, describing the Auckland isthmus in the 1920s and 30s. The top of the North Island, with its peninsulas and drowned valleys, its wide estuaries penetrating deep into the coastline – 'this tousled, sunny-mouthed, sandy-legged coast' as Curnow called it, possesses a summertime subtropical sensuality which is emblemised by its exuberant vegetation – particularly its pohutukawa and its mangroves.

For Kendrick Smithyman the waves breaking on the coastal rocks in 'Where Waikawau Stream Comes Out' is a 'romantic instant of joy', the effect operatic, balletic, as waves smash 'superbly white, crystal sharp, sibylline …'. Allen Curnow, meanwhile, is admiring the pohutukawa tree in blossom on the cliffs above: '… the single/ Actress shuffling red petals to this music/ Percussive light!' Playwright Bruce Mason, however, senses a melancholy in these red flowers: 'The red is of a dying fire at dusk, the green faded and drab'. Picturesque the pohutukawa may be but, as Sarah and Edward Featon hymned in their 1889 *Art Album of New Zealand Flora*, it's also 'Grim, gaunt, weird/ Adorned with strange fantastic arms … It stands:

a silent beacon/ To departing Shades …'. Their poetic conceit rhymes with that of Albert Wendt in his poem 'Te One-Roa-A-Tohe', in which he writes of spirits leaping 'into the prophetic current that will carry them to Hawaiki' from the Northland headland of Te Reinga, where gnarled pohutukawa cling to the cliffs.

Historian Keith Sinclair's autobiography *Halfway Round the Harbour* (1993) describes his childhood at Auckland's Point Chevalier, at that time still semi-rural: 'In those days each summer was forever. Life was the sparkling sea, the dark light under the mangroves, the tide pouring up or down the channel, the heat, the harsh sun'. Mangroves are present somewhere in the background of almost all Northland and Auckland writers. Sometimes they're foregrounded, as by A R D Fairburn in 'The Estuary': 'and the floating shells,/ … still shoreward glide/ … among the mangroves on the creeping tide …'.

Fairburn is the seeker after innocence – his Auckland's a perpetual idyll, not just a protracted adolescent infatuation but a state of mind to cherish forever: 'I could be happy … roaming … I would live on the land, live off it'. His is the old pastoral dream turned escapist, footloose, lyrical:

In summer we rode in the clay country
the road before us trembling in the heat
and on the wind the scent of the tea-tree

Fairburn's art enacts Anthony Trollope's philosophical observation, made after staring at the Marlborough hills: 'The sweetest charms of landscape are as those of life; they consist of the anticipations of something beyond, which can never be reached'.

Maurice Shadbolt's *A Touch of Clay* (1974) celebrates the

rituals of summer, but with the prosaic preoccupations of the storyteller searching for how Auckland's 'warm latitudes', its bays and inlets and humid climate, mould his central character, a potter: 'Summer again, true summer. Thick heat. Manuka and kanuka flowering, frosting those mostly drab trees, and dry clay cracking underfoot …'.

C K Stead's novel, *The Death of the Body* (1986), finds an image for the umbilical connection between people and land in the form of a downpour from the vast, overcast Auckland sky:

Saturday morning, early December. The air hot, heavy, humid and still, the sky darkening until it breaks with a single crack like a starting pistol. The rain comes down very precisely, the single clear drops bouncing on the warm roadway as if they were hailstones … the drops get bigger, then very big … The rustle of water everywhere running like crowds gathering or scattering, gets louder … the drumming on the iron roofs becomes a continuous roar. Only the thunderclaps speak above it.

Further south, rain wind and snow are climatic constants, place markers. Hone Tuwhare, poet of the elements, notices rain 'making small holes in the silence'. Kirsty Gunn at Lake Taupo word-paints rain:

When the rain came it came first as the scent of rain, the grey air stained darker behind the hills. Then when it came down to us it was like thread and needles, piercing the jellyish water with a trillion tiny pricks, the silver threads attaching water to sky.

Visiting Wellington in the early 1960s, British writer Jan Morris was impressed by the winter winds which 'spring rasping out of the Antarctic, scurry and scour through the hilly

streets of the capital, and so shake the frames of the wooden houses that you feel yourself to be actually at sea'.

Poet John Newton, growing up in the South Island, apostrophises the powerful character of the Canterbury nor'wester: 'When the norwest blows/ nowhere is secret from it …'.

Meantime, above the dry basin of Central Otago is, as James K Baxter rapturously acknowledges, 'the wind that blows/ Forever pure down from the tussock ranges'. This pure wind however, according to Charles Brasch in his poem 'The Silent Land' mocks the townsfolk on the plains; like Newton he sees something maddening and revelatory in the high country thermals: 'Beside the sprawling rivers, in the stunted township,/ By the pine windbreak where the hot wind bleeds'.

After wind, snow. Snow is like a folk-memory, a reference point. It falls infrequently on the lowlands, but sometimes unrelentingly. Snow falls over Dunedin City in 1939 in Christine Johnston's novel *Blessed Art Thou Among Women* (1991) 'heavier than anyone could remember … blankets of snow'. Lady Barker is socked in by snow in 'the great snow storm of 1867':

The snow continued to fall in dense fine clouds, quite unlike any snow I ever saw before … It was wonderful to see how completely the whole aspect of the surrounding scenery was changed; the gullies were all filled up, and nearly level with the downs; sharp-pointed cliffs were now round bluffs; there was no vestige of a fence or gate or shrub to be seen, and still the snow came down as if it had only just begun to fall …

The landscape, then, deals in extremes. Danger always lurks for the unwary. Here's Samuel Butler on trying to cross a South Island river:

The stream was wide, rapid and rough, and I could hear the smaller stones knocking against each other under the rage of waters, as upon a seashore. Fording was out of the question. I could not swim and carry my swag, and I dared not leave my swag behind me …

Jane Mander's *The Story of a New Zealand River* (1920), set on the inner Kaipara Harbour in Northland, conveys a vivid picture of the dangerous life led by kauri tree-fellers as they winch logs with steam engines out of the forest, and it also expresses the on-going ambivalence felt about the bush:

From the mangrove banks to the sky a great variety of trees in fifty shades of evergreen covered every yard of space. There was a riotous spring colour in the forest, voluptuous gold and red in the clumps of yellow kowhai and the crimson rata … [but] the first thing that had struck Alice about it all was its appalling isolation. Every mile of it meant a mile further from even such limited civilisation as she had just left behind.

John Mulgan's *Man Alone* confirms one post-settler response to New Zealand's atavistic landscape, that craggy-chasmed terrain of the interior. For Mulgan's Johnson this inland is a place of psychological unease and dread, a purgatory to be endured:

He came at length to what he knew must be the heart of it all, Onetapu … And there he seemed to be caught in something that was wild and furious and stronger than himself … the … sighing and moaning of the wind and sand [was] more mournful and more frightening than anything human that he had known.

Johnson's journey along the Desert Road up onto the Volcanic Plateau and across the Ruahine Ranges to the Kaimanawa Ranges is a key episode in New Zealand's frontier mythology. Johnson is rebuffed by the savage landscape, but he hangs on, he comes through. It's another step into coming to terms with place. Yet the brooding landscape, the power in those geological blocks uplifted, somehow seems to support and confirm the violence, the body heat, the primal rage of works by Keri Hulme (*the bone people* – 1984), Alan Duff (*Once Were Warriors* – 1990), Owen Marshall ('Coming Home in the Dark' – 1995) and Maurice Gee (*Loving Ways* – 1996). Something in the landscape? Something in the water? Something in the soil? In his story 'Coming Home in the Dark', Marshall places random violence and murder, which seem familiar, half-expected, in an indifferent landscape: 'Windswept to a bowl of peerless blue, the sky arched above it all; not oppressive on the landscape, but rather an insistent suction that offered to remove everything into the endless, spun abstraction'.

Writer and farmer W H Guthrie-Smith, though, as he explains in his master-work *Tutira: The Story of a New Zealand Sheep Station* (1921) wanted to study and understand the landscape, he wanted, in Bill Pearson's phrase, 'to make friends' with the landscape. A close-up, finely-tuned, minutely detailed investigation of a sheep station in Hawkes Bay, *Tutira* reveals Guthrie-Smith, a Scottish migrant, to have been a self-taught naturalist and swamp-botanist of obsessive brilliance. He cultivated and studied his 60,000 acre block of land for over half a century. He sought to reach an accommodation between the exotic and the indigenous which was close to worshipful: 'A fence-line can be erected to the glory of the Lord as truly as a cathedral pile'. Guthrie-Smith was an enlightened, ecologically-aware settler. Frank Sargeson, in his autobiography *Once is Enough* (1973) presents the more typical viewpoint of a Waikato hill-farmer, just trying to get by in the raw back-country, using ingenuity and brute strength: 'the little sawmill (was) not much more than a roof supported on upended logs, with much bigger logs bedded into the ground to take the weight of machinery'. Landslides, flooded creeks, mineral deficiencies – trying to coax grass to grow on lifeless topsoils in buckled, twisted country required powers of endurance and a certain grim, resigned humour. This attitude is also found in Frank S Anthony's *Follow the Call*, a series of stories written in the 1920s about a laconically humorous, Fred Dagg-ish, Taranaki farmer:

After leaving the valleys the track crawled up a steep cliff, at an impossible grade of one foot in about four. That's only a guess, however. I've heard old pioneers in their cups refer to that hill as one in two, but I'm inclined to think they were biased.

A sardonic response to the trials of the landscape has always been an undercurrent in the river of New Zealand literary narratives. In 1902 in 'Song of the Gumfield', William Satchell was writing with pointed realism about the atmosphere of the kauri gumlands:

In the scrubby, grubby North when the giddy sun is set,
And the idiot-owl-cicada stops the whirring of his drum,
And the night is growing thicker and the bottled candles flicker,
And the damned mosquitoes bicker in a diabolic hum …

Greg O'Brien, more whimsical, produced this in his 1989 novel *Diesel Mystic*:

Dargaville leans against the Northern Wairoa River, a town fossicking among mangroves and broken carbodies. It is as if the town fell off the back of a bicycle and its absence was not noticed until miles later. And no one could be sure where the town was dropped …

Ronald Hugh Morrieson, by adding local colour – the spirit of Taranaki gothic – to the standard-issue pulp crime novel, created a potent homebrew of Kiwiana in his novel *Came A Hot Friday* (1964). His exuberance gets beneath the quiet provincial facade of a small Taranaki country town in the 1940s and 1950s to reveal the seedy side, the subversive side, of the frontier mentality that lingers from the days of the fiercely fought New Zealand Land Wars of the nineteenth century. He also offers a hint of what had become of the marginalised Maori: 'The road ended in Te Whakinga. It might be more apt to say it threw up its hands in horror and disappeared. Te Whakinga had fallen on evil days. The atmosphere was of decay, melancholy …'.

But by now Maori were beginning to write themselves into the picture. Pakeha writers of the second, third and fourth generations were aiming to show the land as a place where people lived, aiming to show the existence of at a least a version of that pastoral bliss promised by Captain Cook and Edward Gibbon Wakefield. Maori, however, were already living in harmony with the land. Witi Ihimaera's novels always refer back to the philosophical basis: the mana of the land. His home territory is the East Coast, a place of the collective farming of landblocks, organised by Sir Apirana Ngata at the beginning of the twentieth century to help prevent break-up and dispersal of the tribal lands. Ihimaera gives us the sense of a village and a community – an always existing pastoral order:

Waituhi. It was the close kinship the whanau shared with one another. It was the place of the heart. This place of people growing older … This place where the tribal dead slept in the final resting of the body. This place, this Waituhi was family.

Patricia Grace confirms the same Arcadian view of Waiariki,

a coastal community on the west coast of the lower North Island. These writers present their vision as a model, as a 'lesson in place'.

Keri Hulme goes further. She rejects the settler myth of New Zealand as a new Eden, with its Anglocentric, imported emphasis, and proposes a new purity of purpose by placing Maori values at the centre. She proposes a kind of romantic nationalism, which begins, sensibly with ecology: not the destruction of nature (and here she echoes William Pember Reeves in his lament 'The Passing of the Forest') – where pine plantations 'start a chain back from the verge and march on and on in gloomy parade' – but a replanting of the indigenous, the heightened awareness of New Zealand as a green ark.

By contrast, in Alan Duff's version of things Maori, the dispersal of Maori into the general population and intermarriage has meant loss of contact with the land and tradition, and a self-destructive turning inward in the squalor of housing estates. Duff's people practise a kind of historical amnesia. Duff sees not the adoption of the Maori metaphysic and the browning of New Zealand culture as the answer, but rather the re-adoption of the pre-bicultural policy of assimilation. Duff's iconic Pine Block is an economically flattened site, a human scrapheap – a culturally loaded 'wasteland', echoing Edward Gibbon Wakefield's culturally loaded 'waste lands' of first contact.

Raising your head over the roofs and backyards of disempowered Pine Block, however, and the splendour of the land is still there, to be contemplated at dawn or sunset. Poet Graham Lindsay stands on a hill in Havelock North delighting in a view of: 'Amner's great lime block in the orange altocumulus'. In *Tangi* (1973), Witi Ihimaera loads the rifts of landscape with ore: 'a tree already drips gold from the sun and the blossoms catch fire. The sea burns'. Cilla McQueen, gazing inland from Lake Waitaki in south Canterbury murmurs with artistic satisfaction: 'the hills are sleepy moths in the afternoon'. Her reverie is echoed by Keri Hulme's joy on evenings at Okarito Lagoon in early Spring when

… the sunsets are acid-dream vivid, burnt orange and lime green, every shade of pink and maroon and scarlet with piles and bands of navy blue or silver clouds, and the sea gone weirdly pale jade. The lagoon will turn jet black or abruptly fluoresce an unholy bright gold.

Ruth Dallas rhapsodises over the fields of Southland in summer, over the 'ankle-tapping, feathery, heavy-headed grass … Rippling to a feather's passing'. In the tradition of the settlers, she draws precepts from the land, but her sermons are joyous, she is at home here now, all her imagery grows out of place: 'white dust/ Upon green leaves as innocent as snow'. Dust and dry grass. Owen Marshall eulogises the passing seasons, too: 'I love the accumulated heat of the Canterbury autumn. When you rest on the ground you can feel the sustained warmth coming up into your body, and there are pools of dust like talcum powder along the roads'. We have arrived, you can hear these writers saying. We know where we are. Our purchase may be precarious, as in Alistair Campbell's poem 'At the Fishing Settlement', in which he sees 'old houses flanking/ The street hung poised like driftwood planking/ Blown together', or it may be planted in a now mythic past, as with Murray Edmond's poem 'Shack', in praise of the simple vernacular dwelling of the pioneer, the drover, the possum-trapper, the holiday-maker, or the poet: 'It would be good to live in a shack/ In inflationary times a shack would be a good place to live …'.

Some writers, seeking images of purity in landscape, immerse themselves in it like mystics. Poet Rachel McAlpine, intoxicated by 'the core of the land/ the blade of the mountain …' tells us '… we should walk naked/ in air so pure'. Brian Turner, in his poem 'High Noon', uses a kind of animist imagery to show how the landscape speaks through him, the humble shaman of place: 'At the river's edge/ I kneel, then wade in./ The water pushes into my mouth/ a thickening tongue'. Trixie Te Arama Menzies' 'Watercress' is a similarly heightened engagement: 'Burnt gorse and manuka and a cabbage tree/ With the first peel of thunder we were knee-deep in mud and watercress/ We filled our kit, letting the rain soak us …'.

Others have heard the beat of the land's 'oracular heart' by walking across it like pilgrims: Mackenzie, Johnson in *Man Alone*, the hero of C K Stead's novel *Smith's Dream* (1971), the swagman Ned Slattery (as told by John A Lee), himself a joyous walking pilgrim). Hone Tuwhare and Graham Lindsay walking in the Maori Land March of 1975; journalist Geoff Chapple trekking from Te Reinga to Motupohe overland, shadowing writer A H Reed who earlier walked from North Cape to Bluff, along the roads. James K Baxter was the pilgrim walking to Jerusalem, to Hiruharama, his burial place. Baxter never grew to be the old man of the mountains, but as a child he holidayed in the high country, and when he grew up he began more and more to practise deep immersion in landscape. He became, as Allen Curnow said, 'Butler's Erewhon-bound traveller, sleeping rough among the terrible mountains, troubled by organ-pipe dreams'. Prodigal, prodigious, Baxter scattered his poems across the landscape and left them to flower there.

Baxter's journey, Baxter's dream, took in the whole panorama. He became the sum of his landscapes, beginning on the Otago coast and then in Dunedin, a small city with its own character – homely and a bit quirky, Scottish to its backbone – and then launching out into post-World War II society to find a New Zealand complacent, in clover, vegetating, bovine – in need of poetic redemption. The weatherboard suburban bungalow had become a shrine of the new domestic sublime – from deep-pile carpets to fully-stocked refrigerators. By the 1950s New Zealand was, as Austin Mitchell later called it, a 'half-gallon, quarter-acre, pavlova paradise'. Wakefield's grid schemes of settlement had borne fruit – a glut of wood, wool, dairy and meat products. Eric Linklater, a British novelist who visited in 1951 declared: 'It is an island of fatness, in snug houses women vied with their neighbours to whip a stiffer, richer cream'. Poet Gloria Rawlinson, wrote of the rattle of milk-tankers in 'The Old Coach Road', 'taking the farm's snowy rillets/ To swell vast torrents of Waikato cream …'.

In the aftermath of Empire, New Zealand's small towns were cocoons – stuffy, decent, plain, each with its floral clock and centennial fountain. Poet M K Joseph, using Blenheim as his example, wrote of 'the odd/ Remote and shabby peace of a provincial town'. Arnold Wall wrote of Christchurch '[Its streets] are closed with shining Alps' – which the city's inhabitants barely bothered to look at. Rural backwater towns were even drearier, as the new primary school teacher realises in Bill Pearson's novel *Coal Flat* (1963), when she arrives at a little West Coast mining settlement: 'In the shadow of a mountain range a forlorn cluster of roofs and a halo of chimney-smoke …'.

Stevan Eldred-Grigg zooms in on the underlying class divisions of the Wakefield Canterbury settlement with his depiction of working class South Christchurch surveyed from the Cashmere hills in *Oracles and Miracles* (1987):

A lava of red oxide iron, dingy yellow wood and rusty orange signs, cracked and broken by the black ciphers of railways, factories, chimney stacks and the great stinking towers of the Christchurch Gas Coal and Coke Company Limited. A magma of peeling paint, flaking iron, cracked linoleum, dusty yards. Lean-tos and asphalt, dunnies and textile mills.

The sense of something repressed, cramped and stilted in the New Zealand townscape can be found throughout the literature. Louis Johnson writes of the Hutt Valley of the 1950s and 1960s:

The weather is established;
It will be wet – or fine –
The houses are all furnished –
In the styles of 'forty-nine.
No need to worry, hurry;
The questionnaires will keep …

British migrant Peter Bland, arriving in the 1950s, felt the same about the Hutt suburbs: 'monotonous and easy to get lost in …'. Another Bland poem finds him at a Wellington city beach observing the popular mood for 'lying vacant/ among bikinied buttocks and cubist hills'.

But small towns could be a paradise in that territory of the heart we call childhood, as Janet Frame proves with *Owls Do Cry* (1957), and in her story 'The Reservoir', where Eden ends at the town's water supply: 'The Reservoir was the end of the world; beyond it, you fell: beyond it were paddocks of thorns, strange cattle, strange farms'. Frame is a laureate of suburbia. Maurice Gee is another. His tract of paradise is located in Henderson, West Auckland, where he grew up, a place he returns to again and again in his fiction, charting the gradual suburbification from wilderness to place of market gardens to

subdivision. You can't go home again, except in memory. Robert Sullivan updates this post-Edenic West Auckland to the 1990s in 'Fantasy in the Avondalé Valley' (the echo of Baxter in the title tells us Sullivan's poem is a mock-pastoral) as a place of 'half-acre plots, shared drives nestling against land agents'/ signs – pictures of townhouses, vehicles zooming and streaming …'.

Auckland, the city of pseudo-tropical ferment, of lurid opulence and gimcrack fantasy – symbolised by the Skytower casino, rising to bombastic heights tackily out-of-scale with surroundings – has an identity problem with which generations of writers have grappled. Mark Twain in the 1890s acknowledged the superb physical location – 'blue bays twinkling and sparkling away into the dreamy distances where the mountains loom spiritual in their veils of haze', and George Bernard Shaw too, when he visited in 1934, found Auckland 'bright, clean, sunny and happy'. But the architecture of Auckland, according to British writer Beatrice Webb, who visited in 1898 was 'extremely ugly and mean', houses were 'unlovely bungalows … small and uninteresting'. 'Respectable' at best. By 1979 Auckland had stretched to include American-style shopping malls, but Janet Frame's fractured narrative *Living in the Maniototo* (1979) calls the local mall, which is the pride of a North Shore suburb, 'a huge windowless pretence'. Rosie Scott portrays in *Feral City* (1992) something amiss in Auckland's swanning after commercial giganticism, with retribution to follow. Tina Shaw in the novel *Birdie* (1996) identifies the soullessness of an anonymous city seeping into its devalued citizens. Albert Wendt's *Black Rainbow* (1992), offers a dystopian, paranoid vision of Auckland, as if its corporate towers are dedicated to deceit and the mirror-glass buildings of the city centre are intended to blind and confuse.

However for poet and novelist Mike Johnson, writing about

the twilight zones of the city in his collection of poems *Treasure Hunt* (1996), the city is a text to be read for clues in an elaborate and perhaps ultimately meaningless game. Johnson positions himself as a pedestrian between the skyscrapers in a maze of footpaths and Escher-like configurations of escalators. 'Landscapes', he writes meditatively, 'are disclosed in the snakes-&-ladders of walking/ and read with the feet alone'. Johnson writes like an exile-on-main street. He gives voice to the perception that the pastoral has been captured by advertising agencies. Wakefield's vision of paradise has been repackaged: nature can be stage-managed. The grand narrative of landscape now gets retold night after night on television – displacing literature's morality. The New Zealand landscape has become the myth of theme-park pastoral progress, celebrated in a multitude of agenda-driven TV commercials. For urban *flâneurs* such as Johnson in his abstract Downtown (and for a whole raft of other writers), power (myth and meaning) has drained out of the contemporary urbanscape, and by extension the surrounding countryside, into the digitally reproduced images of mass media manipulation. Not only is landscape a commodity, landscape as brandscape, but so are the emotions associated with it: all part of the rampant consumer ideology.

Poets now are producing poems like mobile phone monologues, containing ambivalent, enigmatic references to landscape. In his 1990 poem 'Carnival', Gregory O'Brien uses Wellington harbourside preparations for celebrating the sesquicentennial to suggest how the images traditional to poets and other writers have been overhauled and appropriated by the televisual. The 'truckloads of/ golden sand' which were 'once a beach near Gisborne' turn into 'lengths of East Cape blowing amongst the stagehands'. Landscape here has been cut into manipulable fragments and reduced to a kind of advertising spectacular for an adventure playground. It is full of deeply

suspect symbolism. The short story collection *The Veteran Perils* (1990), by Damien Wilkins, published in the same significant year, offers similarly sceptical images, distrustful of a thoroughly mediated landscape: 'The mountains looked like they had been dropped onto a movie set by helicopter'.

And then there are the recent arrivals, able to alert the locals to what they sometimes take for granted or hadn't noticed. In *Leave before You Go* (1998) London-based New Zealand novelist Emily Perkins shows us Auckland through the eyes of a twenty-something English visitor, a neurotic realist, someone whose media reference points re-triangulate this new place. He is shallow, but then so perhaps is the place he is looking at, all surface:

He wonders if the colours of Auckland are reproduced anywhere else – the blacky-green trees, the changing sea, the painted weatherboard houses … And over it all this uncanny light, ultra-defining, exposing everything like a cut-out in front of a screen.

In Kapka Kassabova's *Reconnaissance* (1999) Nadeja is a Bulgarian backpacker offering first impressions of New Zealand: 'Small things are called big names in this country. Streets are avenues, towns are cities, villages are towns. But here shines the most scorching sun over the most immense ocean, here runs the steepest street, here every person has the greatest number of sheep and boats – the country of deficiencies and excesses'. In this one hears echoes of Wakefield's Utopia, of Butler's anti-Utopia, and also echoes of the broken communist Utopian promises of Eastern Europe.

Writers decipher the territory for us. Niuean novelist John Pule shows us a ghetto landscape which is the other side of that weatherboard bungalow dream-home landscape of the 1960s. He shows us the South Auckland suburb of Otara:

... the Pacific Island church is new ... The Otara creek was full of rubbish ... Turning into Preston Road the bus stopped to pick up the Polynesian factory workers. Where the bus stopped further up to drop passengers off there was a great crowd waiting to get into the TAB.

Pule's novel is the story of another wave of migrants adding to the text of landscape, building on what's gone before, affirming the continuity of landscape. The TAB, for example, can be linked to the race-track – part of the view that short story writer Maurice Duggan saw as significant in its drabness in the 1950s: 'The race-course ... had lost ... its summer colour and only inside the track, where a grey ambulance waited and a few men moved, was grass still to be seen, brown and burned by the sun'.

Literature, then, is a kind of compass, helping us find the countryside that was there all the time: ever-constant yet ever-changing, hidden in plain view and turned into revelation by the cadences of a great relay of writers. All of them, in a sense, are seeking the true identity of the land, the original pristine quiddity smothered beneath layers of human modification. Is it to be found in geology or geomorphology or anthropology, or is it in the mantle of vegetation or the profusion of microclimates, or is its essence finally unknowable – forever modified by the attempts at discovery?

C K STEAD ◆ *After the Wedding*

1

After the wedding comparing notes with
Cousin Elspeth and Cousin Caroline
about our childhood bareback riding
on the Kaiwaka farm —

     How, fallen with your
10-year legs did you get back up
even supposing he stood for you?

Cousin E remembered vaulting from the back
of her pet pig.
        I used the ruts worn deep
by the cream sledge — stood him in the hollow
and leapt from its edge.
        Elspeth
and her sister, blond babies
under the trees I climbed —
      wooden verandah
hot dry garden sheltered by macrocarpa
dogs panting in shade
        my face black
from the summer burn-off.

2

In sleep I still trace those tracks
below gum trees
        skirting the swamp
through bush to that pool of pools
where the small brown fish suspend themselves
in shafts of light.
        My feet sink
midstream in heaped silt
clouding the flow.

      Water had cut its way
through black rock greened with moss
down to that glassy stillness overhung
with trees.

     In the rock cleft
a deep hole water-worn and cold and dark —

I caught the eel that lived there
      its sinuous spirit.

3

In recollection summer is forever
renewing itself even in the thickest
leafmould shade.

        It draws a life
from heat in the ploughed field
where I gathered fossil gum
                or in the hayfield
or in sunlight above the flame
above the dam.

        Cousin Elspeth, Cousin Caroline
cantered bareback
                      fell
(years after me) from the same horse.

4

Weddings are full of God and the word of God
and the word God. I wonder what they mean.
To be one with your body, your body one with the world —
more than a marriage, it's a consummation
bracken and oil-flame like red cellophane
flapping on the hill-slope.
                Eden
won't ask you back, you must make your way
in dreams, by moonlight, or by the broad light of day.

5

There was another stream, a creek
on the far side of the road
where the old house had been.
        It ran through reeds
silent.

The moons repeat themselves
the moreporks retort
the eel and its sibilants
are fluent
           an old chimney stands.

6

It's not what the landscape says
but the way it's said which is a
richness of saying, even of the thing
said —

        that finely articulated slope
a few words at the water
the breathy manuka and the precise
pernickity ti tree

        a long last sentence of cloud
struck out by the dark.

After the wedding
I lie in darkness
I see something that might be myself
        step out for a moment.

It makes the moon
look at itself in water
        it makes the stars
gaze.
    It hears a nightbird and something
        that rustles
in reeds.

It sees itself called
    to light up a silent
vast
     beautiful
            indifferent
waste —

mirror to the mystery
mirrored.

7

Break it
    (the mirror)

the Supreme Intelligence
is always silent
         and death will come
in the guise of just this stillness
or another
      but that was always the case.

8

'Marriages are made in Heaven'
                — not so.

We marry to be nearer the earth
cousins of the fur and stalk
          talking together

that brown water reflecting
those green hills.

JAMES K BAXTER ◆ *High Country Weather*

Alone we are born
    And die alone;
Yet see the red-gold cirrus
    Over snow-mountain shine.

Upon the upland road
    Ride easy, stranger:
Surrender to the sky
    Your heart of anger.

Some few yards from the hut the standing beeches
Let fall their dead limbs, overgrown
With feathered moss and filigree of bracken.
The rotted wood splits clean and hard
Close-grained to the driven axe, with sound of water
Sibilant falling and high nested birds.

In winter blind with snow; but in full summer
The forest blanket sheds its cloudy pollen
And cloaks a range in undevouring fire.
Remote the land's heart. Though the wild scrub cattle
Acclimatized, may learn
Shreds of her purpose, or the taloned kea.

For those who come as I do, half-aware,
Wading the swollen
Matukituki waist-high in snow water,
And stumbling where the mountains throw their dice
Of boulders huge as houses, or the smoking
Cataract flings its arrows on our path—
For us the land is matrix and destroyer,
Resentful, darkly known
By sunset omens, low words heard in branches;
Or where the red deer lift their innocent heads
Snuffing the wind for danger,
And from our footfall's menace bound in terror.

Three emblems of the heart I carry folded
As charms against flood water, sliding shale:
Pale gentian, lily, and bush orchid.
The peaks too have names to suit their whiteness,

Stargazer and Moonraker,
A sailor's language and a mountaineer's.

And those who sleep in close bags fitfully
Besieged by wind in a snowline bivouac—
The carrion parrot with red underwing
Clangs on the roof by night, and daybreak brings
Raincloud on purple ranges, light reflected
Stainless from crumbling glacier, dazzling snow,

Do they not, clay in that unearthly furnace,
Endure the hermit's peace
And mindless ecstasy? Blue-lipped crevasse
And smooth rock chimney straddling—a communion
With what eludes our net—Leviathan
Stirring to ocean birth our inland waters?

Sky's purity; the altar cloth of snow
On deathly summits laid; or avalanche
That shakes the rough moraine with giant laughter;
Snowplume and whirlwind—what are these
But His flawed mirror who gave the mountain strength
And dwells in holy calm, undying freshness?

Therefore we turn, hiding our souls' dullness
From that too blinding glass: turn to the gentle
Dark of the human daydream, child and wife,
Patience of stone and soil, the lawful city
Where man may live, and no wild trespass
Of what's eternal shake his grave of time.

James K Baxter ♦ *At the Fox Glacier Hotel*

One kind of love, a Tourist Bureau print
Of the Alps reflected in Lake Matheson

(Turned upside down it would look the same)
Smiles in the dining room, a lovely mirror

For any middle-aged Narcissus to drown in —
I'm peculiar; I don't want to fall upwards

Into the sky! Now, as the red-eyed tough
West Coast beer-drinkers climb into their trucks

And roar off between colonnades
Of mossed rimu, I sit for a while in the lounge

In front of a fire of end planks
And wait for bedtime with my wife and son,

Thinking about the huge ice torrent moving
Over bluffs and bowls of rock (some other

Kind of love) at the top of the valley –
How it might crack our public looking-glass

If it came down to us, jumping
A century in twenty minutes,

So that we saw, out of the same window
Upstairs where my underpants are hanging to dry,

Suddenly – no, not ourselves
Reflected, or a yellow petrol hoarding,

But the other love, yearning over our roofs
Black pinnacles and fangs of toppling ice.

KATHERINE MANSFIELD ♦ from *At the Bay*

Very early morning. The sun was not yet risen, and the whole of Crescent Bay was hidden under a white sea mist. The big bush-covered hills at the back were smothered. You could not see where they ended and the paddocks and bungalows began. The sandy road was gone and the paddocks and bungalows the other side of it; there were no white dunes covered with reddish grass beyond them; there was nothing to mark which was beach and where was the sea. A heavy dew had fallen. The grass was blue. Big drops hung on the bushes and just did not fall; the silvery, fluffy toi-toi was limp on its long stalks, and all the marigolds and the pinks in the bungalow gardens were bowed to the earth with wetness. Drenched were the cold fuchsias, round pearls of dew lay on the flat nasturtium leaves. It looked as though the sea had beaten up softly in the darkness, as though one immense wave had come rippling, rippling – how far? Perhaps if you had waked up in the middle of the night you might have seen a big fish flicking in at the window and gone again...

Ah-Aah! sounded the sleepy sea. And from the bush there came the sound of little streams flowing, quickly, lightly, slipping between the smooth stones, gushing into ferny basins and out again; and there was the splashing of big drops on large leaves, and something else – what was it? – a faint stirring and shaking, the snapping of a twig and then such silence that it seemed someone was listening.

Round the corner of Crescent Bay, between the piled-up masses of broken rock, a flock of sheep came pattering. They were huddled together, a small, tossing, woolly mass, and their thin, stick-like legs trotted along quickly as if the cold and the quiet had frightened them. Behind them an old sheep-dog, his soaking paws covered with sand, ran along with his nose to the ground, but carelessly, as if thinking of something else. And then in the rocky gateway the shepherd himself appeared. He was a lean, upright old man, in a frieze coat that was covered with a web of tiny drops, velvet trousers tied under the knee, and a wide-awake with a folded blue handkerchief round the brim. One hand was crammed into his belt, the other grasped a beautifully smooth yellow stick. And as he walked, taking his time, he kept up a very soft light whistling, an airy, far-away fluting that sounded mournful and tender. The old dog cut an ancient caper or two and then drew up sharp, ashamed of his levity, and walked a few dignified paces by his master's side. The sheep ran forward in little pattering rushes; they began to bleat, and ghostly flocks and herds answered them from under the sea. 'Baa! Baaa!' For a time they seemed to be always on the same piece of ground. There ahead was stretched the sandy road with shallow puddles; the same soaking bushes showed on either side and the same shadowy palings. Then something immense came into view; an enormous shock-haired giant with his arms stretched out. It was the big gum-tree outside Mrs Stubb's shop, and as they passed by there was a strong whiff of eucalyptus. And now big spots of light gleamed in the mist. The shepherd stopped whistling; he rubbed his red nose and wet beard on his wet sleeve and, screwing up his eyes, glanced in the direction of the sea. The sun was rising. It was marvellous how quickly the mist thinned, sped away,

dissolved from the shallow plain, rolled up from the bush and was gone as if in a hurry to escape; big twists and curls jostled and shouldered each other as the silvery beams broadened. The far-away sky – a bright, pure blue – was reflected in the puddles, and the drops, swimming along the telegraph poles, flashed into points of light. Now the leaping, glittering sea was so bright it made one's eyes ache to look at it. The shepherd drew a pipe, the bowl as small as an acorn, out of his breast pocket, fumbled for a chunk of speckled tobacco, pared off a few shavings and stuffed the bowl. He was a grave, fine-looking old man. As he lit up and the blue smoke wreathed his head, the dog, watching, looked proud of him.

'Baa! Baaa!' The sheep spread out into a fan. They were just clear of the summer colony before the first sleeper turned over and lifted a drowsy head; their cry sounded in the dreams of little children... who lifted their arms to drag down, to cuddle the darling little woolly lambs of sleep. Then the first inhabitant appeared; it was the Burnells' cat Florrie, sitting on the gatepost, far too early as usual, looking for their milk-girl. When she saw the old sheep-dog she sprang up quickly, arched her back, drew in her tabby head, and seemed to give a little fastidious shiver. 'Ugh! What a coarse, revolting creature!' said Florrie. But the old sheep-dog, not looking up, waggled past, flinging out his legs from side to side. Only one of his ears twitched to prove that he saw, and thought her a silly young female.

The breeze of morning lifted in the bush and the smell of leaves and wet black earth mingled with the sharp smell of the sea. Myriads of birds were singing. A goldfinch flew over the shepherd's head and, perching on the tiptop of a spray, it turned to the sun, ruffling its small breast feathers. And now they had passed the fisherman's hut, passed the charred-looking little *whare* where Leila the milk-girl lived with her old

Gran. The sheep strayed over a yellow swamp and Wag, the sheep-dog, padded after, rounded them up and headed them for the steeper, narrower rocky pass that led out of Crescent Bay and towards Daylight Cove. 'Baa! Baaa!' Faint the cry came as they rocked along the fast-drying road. The shepherd put away his pipe, dropping it into his breast-pocket so that the little bowl hung over. And straightway the soft airy whistling began again. Wag ran out along a ledge of rock after something that smelled, and ran back again disgusted. Then pushing, nudging, hurrying, the sheep rounded the bend and the shepherd followed after out of sight....

The bus turns off the road. Nadejda opens her eyes and the sunlight pierces her temples. They have entered a parking lot, swarming with cars and tourists. She looks around. Her co-travellers are moving in their seats, searching for cameras under layers of spread-out maps and bags. Nadejda searches for her sunglasses but her luggage is a mess: they could be anywhere. The passengers trickle out of the bus, armed with cameras and sunglasses. Nadejda can't find her camera either. She doesn't want to take a break or go sightseeing, but she joins the sheeplike column. Follow the column, clutch the camera, croon in a chorus of admiration, get your money's worth, eat your lunch, converse seriously with some Germans, laugh with some Australians, listen to some startling native birds, rock in the coma of crystalline waters, climb the bus steps again following the sturdy bottom of some Dane, and forget everything else in the easy Pacific sun. There's nothing else. How could there be anything else? Sofia pops like a soap bubble.

Nadejda crosses the parking lot towards the sightseeing spot, a still invisible mass of vociferous water. The bus driver unwraps a sandwich: 'It's one hell of a waterfall', he says. Nadejda smiles and nods as if they've been talking about this waterfall all day and now finally she gets to see it. Perhaps they have. Perhaps the driver has been telling the attentive passengers all about it, and she missed everything. Waterfall, of course! Of all natural phenomena, Nadejda has a predilection for waterfalls. She catches a glimmer of unnatural blue through the shrubs lining the riverbank. The thump of water muffles all other noise; a dazzling fury of bluish foam fills her senses. She sets foot on a bridge.

As she crosses the deafening chaos of water, Nadejda sways. She sways but doesn't fall. Why doesn't she fall? Perhaps because the bridge is wide. Perhaps because Nadejda never falls except in dreams. In dreams she falls off crumbling cliffs, concrete staircases, chalet roofs, but especially from bicycles on tight-ropes. Why does she sway now, she who can walk along a banister in her sleep? Because she is not really crossing this river – this river is a conspiracy which her mind has suddenly stopped believing. She is crossing an altogether different river. She keeps walking, swaying, her eyes fixed on the luminous froth below. The thumping noise gives away the real identity of the river.

Nadejda walks inside a dark loophole and comes out the other end where *lush greenery mourns beheaded naked bodies whirling about in the river for centuries. Giant arches bend over the dark water that knows too much. There is no protection here, no signs, no guides, no lunch break. If you stand on that giant back of stone, carved to perfection by ancient waters, there are no railings to protect you. There is no bungy jumping here, at Chudnite Mostove, the Wondrous Bridges. There is something else, though. Nadejda is standing high up on the cliffs. The river rages below. On the other side appear horsemen with fezzes and yatagans, static but vicious, overlooking some punishment. Then, in the early morning mist, she distinguishes a long column of women, men and children, moving towards the cliff.*

'Move, move, you dirty giaours!' says one of the horsemen,

clearly the chief.

Nadejda zooms up to his face – nasty though imposing green eyes, dark moustache, unusually handsome face with a sensuous mouth. He has raped thirty-eight girls and women since he became governor of this region. As the first man in the convoy reaches the edge of the cliff, the green-eyed horseman shouts, perhaps in Bulgarian, perhaps in Turkish; in any case Nadejda understands: 'Will you convert to the Muslim faith?'

The moustachioed man in rags says in a deep, solemn voice, 'Never'.

Only now does Nadejda notice that his hand is missing. The torn white sleeve is drenched with darkness. One swift metallic flash of a yatagan sends his head flying off. He tumbles down, crashing on the sharp rocks. The river embraces him and, swelling his white shirt into a bubble, sets him asail in the wake of his head.

Next comes a young woman with long dark hair. Her dress is torn at the top, her white bare shoulder catching the sun, she stands proud and unflinching. The horseman asks her, in a slightly altered voice (for he has enjoyed her many times): 'Will you convert to the Muslim faith, Kalinna?'

Kalinna spits in his direction with all the strength of her wrecked body and leaps off the cliff. She falls like a white kite, her dress spreading in mid-air. When she hits the water, her face remains a blur carried by the fast frothy stream. It's a body chasing another body.

Back through the loophole, and now Nadejda is on the other bank of the river. Fine spray tickles the air. Instead of savage horsemen and a human row of pain, there are tourists with cameras and sandwiches on this side, all headed down in the direction of the falls. She has just come out of a cinema and must get accustomed to reality. Chudnite Mostove vanish. But what *is* reality? The Huka Falls, she guesses. A crowd flocking at the railing by the falls, this is reality – tons of mindless crystalline water flowing ad infinitum.

Nadejda leans over and watches the effervescent orgy of water. She thinks how it is so unlike the violence of men. Water takes you when nobody else wants you. Sometimes she takes you by force, before you are ready. Sometimes she comes to you, in big mighty crashing waves. She breaks you, then she soothes you. This is a country of water, surrounded by ocean, punctuated by lakes, waterfalls and rivers. This country is rocked by the latent violence of water....

There is a place in the hills where no one wins farmer of the year; high up where the road is still unsealed and has bulges on its length occasionally so that if you're unlucky enough to meet something coming the other way, it can be decided by eye contact and gross tonnage who will back down – and then back up. Much of the land has beaten its proprietors, and so is given over to pine forest, and if the stands are immature the pruned branches are rust filagree beneath the velvet green of the firs. The farm houses are weatherboard and the sheds mainly shot. The dogs are kennelled in a gully head where the mutton bones go to die, and the white leghorns flap up into nooks of the equipment shed to roost, where they mute on the harnesses and the post-hole digger which have no other use. There are boxes and bags of apparently unused seed, but the birds and the mice have long since been in and all can be winnowed away. There's a tractor seat cover made from possum pelts and stirrup pumps that have never worked and refuse to start doing so now. In the shearing shed the wood is richly stained with fleece oil and dags and a little blood and sweat. A track winds over the gorse-covered top of the gully to the manuka country beyond and slopes of pigfern rooted over by the namesake, and screes of serpentine rock which make a cheap fence because the sheep will hardly cross, and a high pond or two which you'd never know were there, but the stock tracks wind their way to them and the mallards which can be covered with a couple of guns. Pretty much dry country most of the time, and the hack still better than the farm bike, but there are days when the cloud comes in, the gorse and briar glisten almost as much as the serpentine, the manuka stems gradually darken as the rain seeps through, the pigfern is bowed down by the weight of the drops it bears.

There are ridges and faces and gullies and spurs that don't appear on maps. They're given names by the family who have to climb them and when the people go they take away the names. There's a place where beech were sledded down to make the first houses and there's a place in the creek, a small falls, where the biggest boar was stuck, whose tusks hang over the shearing shed and glint in the evening sun. No matter who does the muster, no matter how keen the dogs, there are a few old woollies on every place that never come down to the yards. But you know all that.

There's a place, not far, sweet country if only it had summer rain. The sheep seek shade, and in these camps the loess clay of the ground is smooth and hard, or pooled to dust, and the droppings of the sheep are thickly spread, but dry and inoffensive, baked in the heat. In the odd sink hole the briar seeks moisture and gorse blooms brighter than the clay. The ridges are worn almost bald, like the heads of the lean, brown farmers who ride farm bikes too small for them across the paddocks of their land. The creek beds are marked more by rushes and willows than running water, and the mallards come only in twos or threes. An easterly is always up after midday and burnishes the arc of pale, blue sky. The shelter belts close to the road and the macrocarpa before the farmhouse, are dusted with a false pollen drifting in off the road. The rural delivery boxes are large so that stores can be left there as well as mail, and each has a name painted by hand. In the evenings the sheep come to the stock dams and troughs to drink, the magpies gather to imitate the noise of poets, and the barley grass and brown-top ripple at the sides of the shingle roads.

Is that so far away?

ELIZABETH KNOX ◆ from *When We Stopped*

The roadsides we see passing through are a litany, especially roads we know to places we love. Highway dust over all the Rai Saddle forest, clouds of nerve gas, yellow pine pollen; the ragged spume of grass, blurred as we pass, a foamy wake falling behind us. To stop is a celebration, a quartered orange in a rest area, Mass, half-time in a rugby game. Even a busy stop is, somehow, like silent prayer, contemplation. Even the high street of Buller where we stopped to have tea and filch salt and pepper from the cruet set on our table—we were camping and had none—even the dullest places declare themselves deep after all those rapids

We had winter holidays. Driving up to Waikaremoana in two cars—the Knoxes and Johns—I rode with Daph, Olaf and Robin. We were in the lead, driving sedately, we had seen Dad pull over, probably so Mary could be sick or walk off nausea. They hadn't reappeared. It was 1975, Robin and I were listening to her tape of *Yellow Brick Road*, to my anthem, the all-out, grandstanding sentiment of 'Don't Let the Sun go Down on Me'. Teenagers—always rehearsing for oblivion, as though adulthood is oblivion. *Sure.* Some few months later a friend went to lengths we morbid throat-clearers didn't—four feet approximately, of taut rope.

Daph saw the feral goat caught in a fence. We did a U-ee and drove up on to the rest area above the road. Olaf crossed the highway and stood assessing the goat. It plunged and struggled as he approached then stilled and simply watched, its yellow eyes trapdoors open a slit on a dark attic.

Robin and I were told to watch for Dad and wave him down. I had my first look at the rough hills up the back of Hawke's Bay: pasture, not of the King David variety, but an undistinguished green, thistles, scrubby hills silvered by that mid-North Island light, not quite as clear as the light at Cook Strait, or the white anvil of Hauraki Auckland smokes on. So many hills, such badly trampled land (you could still hear Maui telling his brothers, 'Let it set'.) To me the land was a prodigy, so many thicknesses of landforms, and no sea in sight. These were ordinary circumstances, I was just seeing some place for the first time, but the appearance of the ocean in almost all extensive views is essential to this country. It didn't occur to me at the time, but that view – Olaf and the goat in its foreground – is exhibit A of my evidence, my evidence for a case. Good visibility, few mists, a couple of skinny islands – when we have done enough travelling in our country we develop, perhaps, very fine proprioception (the brain's map of the body), and even blinded, or balance-disturbed, we are still in touch with our toes. Our hinterland isn't a great space but 'up the back of there', where lost herds of hairy black bog cattle hide, and the bush is so thick it flattens into a wall – green, with black espaliered supplejack – everyone's back fence....

BASIL DOWLING ◆ *Canterbury*

On this great plain the eye
Sees less of land than sky,
And men seem to inhabit here
As much the cloud-crossed hemisphere
As the flat earth. Trains travel fast and straight,
And travellers early or late
Think of their destination
More than of pasture, wheatfield, wayside station.
Here birds and winds fly free,
And tree is miles from tree
Except where in dark ranks they muster
Against the gales or cluster
Befriending lonely farms.
Tired tramps and trampers fare
Sadly along the endless roads, but the hare
Is lucky, and the magpie, black and white
Highwayman with his shout.
Sounds are soon dead being echoless

In the vast emptiness,
Though thunder and the ocean roar
Carry, on calm days, far:
And some sounds hardly ever rest:
The sound of wind from nor'east or nor'west
And three great rivers with proud Maori names
Chafing worn shingle till the ocean tames
Their wildness. This is my holy land
Of childhood. Trying to comprehend
And learn it like the features of a friend,
Sight rides on power-poles and tops of trees
From the long eastern beaches and loud seas
League after league
Till definition fades in bluish vague
Distance: then dreams begin
To see in vision colourless and thin
Beyond the western foothills lost
The huge and desolate ranges of the Coast.

RUTH DALLAS ◆ *In Central Otago*

Seek foliage and find
Among cracked boulders
Scab of lichen, thyme.

Seek a burgeoning tree
Discover
Upended witches' brooms.

Seek grass and tread
Stiff sheet of ice drawn
Over the land dead.

Moon country.
No one could live here,
In the houses squat on shingle.

Fields scorched,
Snow gripping the mountains;
Nothing could recover

From such desolation,
Jack Frost's sheep-run,
Mirror of the bleak mind.

But come back in a month –
See blanketing the slits
And sockets of the land's skeleton

Square eiderdowns of peach-bloom,
Old crone, Plum, unpick
A feather mattress from a bald stone.

JOHN MULGAN ◆ from *Man Alone*

His brain was working clearly again as he moved against the weight of wind and rain, and he knew what was against him. He had heard men talk of how sometimes prisoners broke from the camp across the mountain and took to the bush. Then it was like a game to the prison guards, a game that they usually won. They picketed all the bridges and cross-roads and searched the mountain huts; after that they waited for the rain that always came to drive the fugitives out of the bush to them. He had on his side some food and an ability to last them out, but that was all.

He had a hard day, going these few miles round the mountain-side. He was forced up, higher and higher, in an attempt to avoid the deep, stone valleys that ran between ridges, steep and impassable, until he was up near the snow-line coming on small patches of snow among the rocks. Up here the mist driving against him was often half sleet and very cold on his face and ungloved hands. He forced his way on, going as well as he could, and trying to keep his general direction by the slope of the ridges, a journey made hard by broken, ice-worn rock and the heavy pack he carried. The weather cleared for a little while in the late afternoon so that he could see the sharp peak they called Girdlestone above him and could get his line before the mist came down again. He made his way down then, judging himself to have come far enough round the mountain, until he found the edge of tussock again. The bush died away here, on this side of the mountain, into small isolated clumps of trees breaking the stone and tussock. When night fell he dug himself into the loose pumice soil and slept

with the sound of wind in his ears, and rain more heavy now, falling over him. It was a cold night, but not unbearable.

He woke to a morning that was just light underneath a sky still black with the storm. The gale had strengthened so that it had reached its height. He knew well from experience the course that it would take. This was the third day of its fury, with heavy rain in the wind now. It would blow like this all day and another night, and rain heavily, with a steady drenching rain, for two days after that, until the wind went round to the west again. He was chilled and wet through and foodless, but the wildness of the weather gave him a chance of escape.

As he went on in the early morning, fearful of losing all direction, but trying to judge the slope of the land as it ran down to the plain, he came to a strange and desolate country. What he saw was a waste of scarred and pitted desert, bare of all growth for long stretches, loose scoria and pumice powdered to sand by years of weathering, and lifting now, as the gale came violently, so that it rose in swirling clouds that wrapped him round and blinded him. Here and there stunted shrubs clung desperately in the shelter of breaks and hummocks in the sand, and the ground was strewn with the charred fragments of old forests wasted by volcanic fire. He had heard men speak of this, too, of the Rangipo desert, the waste area where long before the volcanoes of the mountain had burned and embedded the forests, and the loose volcanic sand, played on by years of driving winds, had given no home for anything to grow. It was a legend-haunted country, dreaded by the Maoris. He could remember them telling him how long

ago the first natives of the country had been driven down here by invaders to die and after that there were stories of Maori tribes caught by snow and starved to death in these same deserts. There had been times when the desert held packs of savage and wandering dogs until they, too, died away in that lifeless area, and it was left as barren and desolate as ever. As he went blindly forward, going doggedly, his head down, barely seeing the ground beneath his feet, he came at length to what he knew must be the heart of it all, Onetapu, the place of the shivering sands. And there he seemed to be caught in something that was wild and furious and stronger than himself. The wind came no longer directly against him, but eddying and whirling in gusts of sand and storm so that he could hardly stand or go forward in any direction. The quiet and silence of the mountain-side was gone and in its place came a sighing and moaning of wind and sand as it stirred in the corridors of the desert, more mournful and more frightening than anything human that he had known. He fought this for a long time, both the feeling of terror and the force of the storm, baffled and angry, going sometimes forward or being swayed to left and right, stumbling and falling, going on his hands and knees, until at last he caught the shelter of a pumice bank and stayed there, burrowed into it, with his back against the shelter and the rain and sand blowing over him. He was exhausted and if snow came, he told himself, ready to die. Night fell and no snow came, but only rain and sand. He ate a little raw flour and oatmeal, moistened into a gritty paste in his hands, and did not sleep, stirring uneasily to keep the circulation in his limbs. With the grey of the morning the wind died and rain came down heavily and gloomily: the day was dark and remained dark with heavy clouds. There was almost no visibility, but it was possible to go forward now and to strike a rough line against the slight drift of the rain. He went on until he came out of the sand and on to tussock again that seemed by comparison alive and healthy...

The clouds lifted a little in the late afternoon and showed him, for the first time, the shadow of the mountain range ahead that was his goal. The steep bush-hills rose up grimly and darkly out of the plain. But they were still farther from him than he had hoped and he spent the night again on the plain with rain still drenching down. He woke this time before it was light, with his limbs shaking and his jaws twitching uncontrollably, his head burning as if with fever. He was frightened then of falling ill, but the feeling went away as he forced himself up and on again, though his head was light; he felt giddy, and the movements of his legs seemed un-coordinated and unreal. He chewed tobacco as he went forward to keep himself from thinking of his hunger and cold....

This was real bush that he was going into now, not the mountain-bush of birch-trees that he had seen on Ruapehu, but deep, thick, and matted, great trees going up to the sky, and beneath them a tangle of ferns and bush-lawyer and undergrowth, the ground heavy with layers of rotting leaves and mould. To go forward at all was difficult, held back all the time by twining undergrowth. The air was dark and lifeless; it was rich with the sweet, rotting smell of the bush, and only stray glimpses of light came through the leaves above. He had only a general and limited sense of direction, but followed the path of a bush creek which wound its way through the bottom of the valley into the heart of the range. He was going deep into this, so deep, he told himself, that he might never come out again. Following the creek bed was difficult and exhausting, but gave some hopes of progress with its occasional short stretches clear of over-growing trees. As he followed it in, going for five days laboriously forward, making at best not more than eight or ten miles each day, the hills seemed to close round and over him until he felt himself to be farther than anyone could ever follow him, surrounded and drowned in the hills and bush, safe and alone and submerged. He had to climb after that to get over the first heights of the range that ran up six thousand feet high, and he did this after two weeks of journeying, going up again to a country of bare rock and lichen and down again to a great valley beyond that fell steeply two thousand feet. The day that he came down again into bush country, snow fell. It lay heavily on the heights behind him and would stay there, he knew, through the winter months that were on them now. Even lower in the valley it covered the trees and lay in patches on the ground. He decided then, that if he were to endure through the next three months he must have warmth and shelter for himself, and stopped then, when he came to the depths of this great valley, to find it....

Yes, what would this man have done had his childhood been different, the *Auckland Star* asked, reviewing my *Simple on a Soapbox*. At seventy-four, I know that had I not run from the police, I should never have seen the Wanganui in its spellbinding forest-clad days. As I arose from my fern bed, I had crossed the Wanganui at Taumarunui and in Wanganui only, which means that the Wanganui revelation had yet to come.

We splashed our faces with water at a small creek and ate. Ned and the Maoris talked and I wondered what was said.

"The Wanganui is about forty yards away," Ned told me.

The bush was heavy, the undergrowth along the river edge was dense. We could neither hear nor see the flowing water. We walked the few yards. We were high above the water as we searched. There was a papa cliff thirty feet high across the river as at the bank on which we stood. The river's edge was fern, tangled undergrowth, tall timber, a few yards back from the edge of the cliff the undisturbed forest of two thousand years. The water below was deep, unrippled. Wanganui magic possessed me as I held back a branch.

"Come," a girl said.

The elders did not move from the whare with us. They had given us shelter and food and had wished us well. The girls had a sense of adventure as they led down a slanting path to the river below. They spoke enough English for my understanding. Years before, some people coming downriver from Taumarunui had left a flat-bottomed punt where they had camped and had gone back upstream on the river boat. The punt was in fairly good order. The Maoris had possessed the

punt and would give it to us and give us a couple of paddles.

We crossed the river in a canoe they dragged into the water, each girl taking a paddle after we looked upstream and downstream to see that no police boat was about. I wonder if the excited girls were as beautiful as they seemed that morning or if they were just part of the Wanganui magic. They paddled across and we dismounted and they drew the canoe out on a shingle shelf.

"This way."

Up another slanting path and along a cliff and the edge of the bush and river for some time and there, where another stream ran to the river, they showed us the punt which they had often used. It was waterproof, for rain had left a few inches of water in its bottom. They dragged the punt to the deep water. There was a tin for bailing. They handed us two paddles, held back undergrowth and watched.

We lingered. We were young and the girls were lovely—native girls against primeval forest on the edge of this inspiring stream. But the police were after us. I am sure we said goodbye and dipped our paddles with sad hearts as the waters moved the punt. The girls held back the branches and watched and waved; we used the paddles only to keep the punt in midstream, and an enchanting moment ended. I am sure the excitement of helping escapers enhanced the loveliness of the girls. The spell of the girls was gone forever, the spell of the river fell upon us.

In those days a boat ran from Wanganui to Taumarunui and people spent a night on a houseboat halfway upstream.

The age was as leisurely as the river flow, people were content to dwell for a day in river worship, internal combustion did not exist to cause folk to want to know mileage when magic was enough.

Advertisements called the river the Rhine of New Zealand. It was not the Rhine nor the low-banked lazy Thames but a unique world's masterpiece created by two thousand years of rain forest, untouched as yet by man, a forest that towered high above high river banks. The steep papa cliffs were covered with fern and moss and creeper and green slime smears. In a hundred places water tumbled over high banks. The river ran slowly except over odd rapids. Misty rains shrouded and unshrouded green hills. For miles the only way to leave the river was up steep banks. The river was neither in high flood nor low as we dipped our paddles, and here and there turns in the river had left dry deposits of shingle and driftwood. The river was no Rhine or Thames or Colorado or Waikato; it was a masterpiece that owed nothing to man. Vegetation, river, wreathing and unwreathing of mists on water and hills, and so quiet, as we drifted, with miles of magic holding the delinquents in a spell that retrospectively can hypnotise until this day. Tall banks, deep twisting canyons that at places made the papa walls give ten-fold in echo, the river incomparable.

"Hello!" We tried the echo to hear our voices return.

"Hello! Hello! Hello!"

Never did humans have such need to search upstream and downstream for a police launch that might move around a bend. Never did locality so completely obliterate concern for police. I sat in front, Ned, as befitted his Maori skill, held paddle in the rear lest we round a placid bend and find the punt gripped by speeding shoal waters. Oh Wanganui, how you generously bestowed two thousand years of preparation upon two escapers!

Ned loved that river as I did—should not the word be venerated? Ten thousand times I could call him to see the beauty ahead as I sat toward the stem, and ten thousand times would he call to me to see the magic we were leaving behind. Each bend was a new unfolding, each breath of air that tore mist from this hill and enfolded that. Oh, that I could have seen the departing scene as well as the coming, as we committed ourselves to the stream, using paddles only to keep us in midstream or to keep stem pointing downstream.

For half a century I have had ambition to drift downstream again from Taumarunui, but the forest that came to the edge, the bird-filled forest is no longer there, so maybe it is better that I keep the memory of beauty primeval in my heart. It is never the same if you go back. Too many hills are bared of giants above Pipiriki.

Gone are the forest birds, arboreal things,
Eaters of honey, honey-sweet of song.

I cannot go back lest I no longer discover a spellbinding masterpiece, but rather where once was "the fire's black smirch" I discover "the landscape's gaping wound". And if I did go back, no excited Maori girls of what then seemed a bush beauty would be there to hold back the branches and watch us go. Would there be branches for them to hold back? Because I was a delinquent I slept on the bosom of river beauty which took thousands of years to create, and a quarter of a century to lay waste. I know that the people who listed the seven wonders of the world never saw the Wanganui a Maori and myself possessed. No wonder that in spirit I have ever been a New Zealander. I possessed the river but never a Maori girl, although my father had children by the daughter of a quite famous chief, but of that some other time....

The block first handled consisted of about 1600 acres of fairly good conglomerate land. The preliminary step was to get it burnt – not always an easy job, for it has always been impossible to be sure of a prolonged spell of drought on Tutira. There has been anxiety always lest wet weather should supervene, lest the bracken should not dry sufficiently to ensure a clean burn. With what trepidation, as autumn approached, have we not watched the skies! Not only had the bracken to be dry, but for a perfect burning day an atmosphere of scorching aridity was also required – a cloudless sky. On the particular March morning when we thus burnt out Stuart's paddock for the first time, all went well. A fierce sun blazed uninterruptedly from a sky of deepest blue; thin wisps of cloud, signs of the coming gale, lay high over the Maungaharuru Range. By eleven o'clock – be sure we were on the spot promptly – we were waiting, one eye on our watches the other on the sky, feeling for preliminary puffs of air, handling lovingly the lucifers that would give us black ground, a sward of English grass, increase of healthy stock, and supply a long train of benefits to the beloved station. There we waited in the fern barely restraining ourselves, "calming ourselves to the long-wished-for end," reflecting that every hour, every half hour, every minute of patience, was drying more and more thoroughly the layers of brake piled one on top of another.

What anxieties have I not known during the last hour or so of such a vigil! Supposing the wished-for breeze should fail? Supposing white fleecy clouds should diffuse a deplorable damp? – forebodings dark as those conjured up in a banker's parlour arise in the mind. Supposing – I have known it happen – the sky should become overcast, yet not actually forbid a fire? Suppose there should be the tragic choice of delay – perhaps for a week, perhaps for a month, perhaps for the season? or, on the other hand, a burn disfigured by patches of green, marred by strips and tongues of unburnt stuff, areas of thin fern unconsumed, breaks in the black at every trivial creek and sheep-track, a crestfallen return clouded with misgivings as to the wisdom of having attempted a fire, at not having waited for a better chance?

Upon that March day, however, though, like Elijah, we scanned the sky, no cloud even like a man's hand appeared. Although all went well, and although it might be sufficient to leave it at that, some readers may care to hear the details of such a day – at any rate the writer wishes to remind himself of pleasures past and gone. Towards noon, then, the fateful match is struck, the smoke curls upwards blue and thin, the clear flame, steady at first but soon lengthening and stretching itself, arises like a snake from its cold coils. Then, as often seems to happen, the draught of the fire summons at once the waiting wind; out of the hot calm bursts forth the newborn storm; the circle of flame lengthens into a streak which, widening at every edge, is pounced upon, flattened to the ground, and furiously fanned this way and that, as if in attempted extinction. A few minutes later a line of commingled flame and smoke, moving ahead with a steady roar, sweeps the hillsides.

Few sights are more engrossing, more enthralling, than the

play of wind and flame. Wind in the hills, like water in its course, never for an instant remains even in its force, but ceaselessly swells and fails, waxes and wanes. In the very height of a gale the rushing charge of fire will in an instant check, the flames previously pinned down will erect their forked tongues like a crop, or lift as if drawn upwards from the earth in the very consummation of their burning embrace; the smoke, a moment previously flattened into the suffocated fern, will rise thin like steam through the winged fronds. Upon slopes exposed to greater weight of wind the pace of the conflagration quickens, forked sheets of flame that singe and scorch the shrivelling upper growth reach far ahead; forward the conflagration rolls – sometimes grey, sometimes glowing, sometimes incandescent, according to the changeful gusts. As a lover wraps his mistress in his arms, so the flames wrap the stately cabbage-trees, stripping them naked of their matted mantles of brown, devouring their tall stems with kisses of fire, crackling like musketry amongst the spluttering flax, hissing and spitting in the tutu-groves, pouring in black smoke from thickets of scrub. On the tops pressed forward by the full force of the gale the roaring conflagration passes upwards and over in low-blown whirlwinds of smoke darkened with dust of flying charcoal and lit with showers of fiery sparks and airy handfuls of incandescent and blazing brake. To leeward fire is no less wonderful to watch as it slowly recedes downhill, devouring in leisurely fashion first the driest material, then sapping the stems of the later, greener, still upright fronds, so that they too bow like Dagon and fall to earth, perpetually replenishing the flames. A fire thus fed, burning against the wind or downhill, presents at night-time a peculiar twinkling, winking appearance from the perpetually recurring fall of the green fronds into the blaze, and the consequent alternations of darkness and light.

In windless hollows yet another mood may be noted: there the flames, burning slowly, stretch and dip and curtsey and sway to the draw of the gale above; in the mazes of the magic dance they take their time and measure from the wind, veering now to one point of the compass now to another, sliding and gliding in accompaniment to unseen harps of the air. So, on that afternoon of March, like the waters of Lodore, the fire passed over Stuart's paddock, roaring and pouring, and howling and growling, and flashing and dashing and crashing, and fuming and consuming not only the block so named, but hundreds of acres besides of the Rocky Range – then included in the Moeangiangi run – the whole of the Black Stag, and nearly the whole of the Tutu Faces.

At nightfall, over every acre unswept by the wind lay a delicate grey veil – a light ash of shrivelled fronds still retaining their shape. A tang of salt, as from the ocean, scented the air, whilst here and there on the driest flats rose thin lines of blue from smouldering totara logs. Everywhere the contours of the countryside lay dim; the sard sun, low in the dun horizon, glowed a burning, blood-red ball; like the fog of a great city, a pall of smoke hung over the land....

FIONA FARRELL ◆ from *A Story About Skinny Louie*

THE SETTING

Imagine a small town: along its edges, chaos.

To the east, clinking shelves of shingle and a tearing sea, surging in from South America across thousands of gull-studded, white-capped heaving miles.

To the south, the worn hump of a volcano crewcut with pines dark and silent, but dimpled still on the crest where melted rock and fire have spilled to the sea, where they have hissed and set into solid bubbles, black threaded with red.

To the west, a border of hilly terraces, built up from layer upon layer of shells which rose once, dripping, from the sea and could as easily shudder like the fish it is in legend, and dive.

To the north, flat paddocks pockmarked with stone and the river which made them shifting restlessly from channel to channel in its broad braided bed.

Nothing is sure.

The town pretends, of course, settled rump-down on the coastal plain with its back to the sea, which creeps up yearly a nibble here a bite there, until a whole football field has gone at the boys' high school and the cliff walkway crumbles and the sea demands propitiation, truckloads of rubble and con-crete blocks. And the town inches away in neat rectangular steps up the flanks of the volcano which the council names after an early mayor, a lardy mutton-chop of a man, hoping to

tame it as the Greeks thought they'd fool the Furies by calling them the Kindly Ones; inches away across shingle bar and flax swamp to the shell terraces and over where order frays at last into unpaved roads, creeks flowing like black oil beneath willows tangled in convolvulus, and old villa houses, gap-toothed, teetering on saggy piles, with an infestation of hens in the yard and a yellow-toothed dog chained to the water tank.

At the centre, things seem under control. The Post Office is a white wedding cake, scalloped and frilled, and across the road are the banks putting on a responsible Greek front (though ramshackle corrugated iron behind). At each end of the main street the town mourns its glorious dead with a grieving soldier in puttees to the north and a defiant lion to the south, and in between a cohort of memorial elms was drawn up respectfully until 1952 when it was discovered that down in the dark the trees had broken ranks and were rootling around under the road tearing crevices in the tarmac, and the Council was forced to be stern: tore out the lot and replaced them with plots of more compliant African marigolds. There are shops and petrol stations and churches and flower-ing cherries for beautification and a little harbour with a tea kiosk in the lee of the volcano. It's as sweet as a nut, as neat as a pie, as a pin.

Imagine it....

HONE TUWHARE ◆ *Kaka Point*

Rain – intermittently – spotting the glass on the eastern
window of my small Crib. Through it in vertical
dominance, stands a wooden power-pole in a wire-
weighted, wire-distributing role, servicing five
neighbourly houses, and mine.

I shall buy a small gas-cooker, together with
a plump, light-green L.P.G. bottle – just in case
there's a power-failure and all the tucker in
the fridge goes off to a new era of decadence.

The view through my window is rectangular, fresh, and
unhurried. Unlike Tee-Vee, the view does not do
your thinking for you. The power-pole is festooned
with a choir of singing wires – a Kiwi Landscape
of classical distinction. Second-rate artists
leave it out of their pictures, altogether.

Way out and beyond, I sense a whole World in movement
and flex. On the same latitude, Chile nudges, just
over the horizon.
And because the Sea is multi-lingual, I share
its collective heart-beat, with all poets, in all
lands, joined together by oceans of applause – and a
fine mutuality of taste, for fish (and chips, please)

With them I share the Seas' broken lines
of white toppings; the curved, green-veined
wave-caverns, like close-bound copper-strands
under a withheld tension – and release; their
height reduced to white, tickle-toe-clenchings
in sand – bach-peddling

Soon – very soon, the Season for shoals of small fish shall
thicken, and – right on time – the Sooty Shearwater
will rendezvous in their tens of thousands filling
the air with their greedy but joyful chatter.
Vast areas of Tangaroa's armpits, shall be darkened
by the ceaseless movement of beak and plumage –
a welter of gourmet-tasters with impeccable table
manners. My hunger and longing is increased: I lift
the phone, and place my order for a modest bucket
of 45 preserved Tii-tii. I refrain from asking for
the price.

Come, Sooty Shearwater, harbinger of good medicinal tucker.
Eat well – and mate well – so that your woolly, roly-
poly progeny will thrive in their thousands for us:
and Amine, to all that.

HONE TUWHARE ♦ *The old place*

No one comes
by way of the doughy track
through straggly tea tree bush
and gorse, past the hidden spring
and bitter cress.

Under the chill moon's light
no one cares to look upon
the drunken fence-posts
and the gate white with moss.

No one except the wind
saw the old place
make her final curtsy
to the sky and earth:

and in no protesting sense
did iron and barbed wire
ease to the rust's invasion
nor twang more tautly
to the wind's slap and scream.

On the cream-lorry
or morning paper van no one comes,
for no one will ever leave
the golden city on the fussy train;
and there will be no more waiting
on the hill beside the quiet tree
where the old place falters
because no one comes any more

no one.

RONALD HUGH MORRIESON ◆ from *Came a Hot Friday*

Every mile that passed, now the Blue Kiwi Tavern bridge was crossed, the loudly purring mobile oven which was the Citroen bore Don deeper into a waste-land of sandhills, gorse and boxthorn, thirty thousand acres of blistering iron-sand, sulking in the shadows of passing clouds, harshly aglitter with a billion sequins in the bright sun, but buried for the most part in the tussock grass and golden-yellow gorse.

Even on the left, stretching away into the blue hills and bush of the hinterland, the rolling farm country, with its pleasant belts of pine and macrocarpa, was beginning to surrender. When the road turned toward and neared the coast, the wilderness reached across the river. Creeks that had struggled as far as this expired in swamps, their headstones in many cases the ancient, barkless trunks of trees lifeless and askew, their wreaths the forlorn plumes of pampas grass. Only a great grey-green battleship like the Apuna river could survive in such enemy territory. The lush gorge, the shadow and reflection of fern and willow left behind like happier days, the Apuna forged its way with sluggish might down to the Tasman Sea.

Soon the road swung away from the river and the long incline into Apuna began; but the township, embalmed, along with its cooked-kidney smell, in the silence of a Sunday morning, made a dubious oasis. Only the big freezing works had promoted Apuna from its natural status, a Maori village at the river's mouth.

The road from the town on was new to Don. It was only a hard, dirt road coated with sand, running between sand-dunes and the wide, wild, driftwood-strewn beach. The coastline at Apuna dipped nearly to sea level, but immediately around the breaker-lashed point the characteristically sheer and rugged cliffs loomed up again. A few hundred yards short of the point, the road turned sharply up into the sand-dunes, narrowed, began to wind, nearly lost its identity as a road altogether. From its ambush in the hills of sharp, angry grass and sand-stifled gorse the heat pounced on the little car like an assassin. The road ended in Te Whakinga. It might be more apt to say it threw up its hands in horror and disappeared. Te Whakinga had fallen on evil days. The atmosphere was of decay, melancholy.

The houses and *whares*, arranged to make three sides of a square hemming in a big *marae* or common, were in a sad state of disrepair. Behind the houses were doorless latrines, tottering like decrepit tombstones and giving the impression of having been moved a few yards to pastures new, time and time again. The meeting-house, the *whare-whakino*, easily distinguished by its length and fearsomely and elaborately carved facade, was in the centre at the very back. Of human habitation there was no sign, not even a witch-doctor in a bone suit. A venerable horse, badly in need of a haircut, had the paddock to himself....

My uncle's land was O.R.P. (Occupation with Right of Purchase), four hundred acres drawn in a Crown Lands ballot in the year 1913: it was tucked away at the narrow top end of a valley that widened out before splitting into a number of tortuous clefts, all of them rising to a great semi-encircling watershed. But my uncle couldn't see his land for the trees, thick and heavy bush that made it quite impossible to know just what the cleared land would look like – although it seemed he would be lucky if he uncovered ground sufficiently level and open to accommodate a decent-sized house. In the meantime he built his hut, but managed after a few years to buy an extra 90 or so acres – freehold Maori land that joined on to his leasehold: it continued down the valley on one side until the valley ran out on a somewhat similar one running at right angles: this new land was very steep mostly, but mostly covered by fern and manuka instead of bush, with perhaps a dozen acres that a hillside plough could be used on; and alongside the creek where it left the valley an acre or two of pumice terrace as flat and suitable for building as you could wish for. And all this latter was after my brother's visit and before my own...

...by the time I first saw the farm: only a few patches of bush that my uncle had decided to keep remained for me to see. It had been as though when he took up his land in the year 1913 he returned to European beginnings in New Zealand a hundred years previously, cramming into seven years a sort of small-scale repetition of his country's history – repeating in his ignorance, as he would later on admit, some of the worst mistakes the pioneers had made. During his beginnings it had just never occurred to him that country so broken might not be suitable for growing grass for sheep; and it still did not occur to him for some years after the bush had been burned. How could it when newly cleared ground, temporarily enriched by potash, would for a season or two grow grass that came up higher than a man was tall? But that too belonged to the past at the time of my first visit. And mistakes apart, it was hard to believe that so much had been achieved in those few years: the entire property had been fenced along its miles of boundary, and intelligently subdivided into about a dozen paddocks of varying sizes, the taut fencelines catching the eye as they angled up the sharp crests of the spurs, or went unangled up those that might be conveniently arrow-straight.

For his first few seasons my uncle had had to shear with the blades, out in the open at the docking yards he had built on the site of the dismantled hauling engine: but soon a woolshed with an oil engine and two stands for shearing, with yards adjoining and shelter trees planted, had been built midway along the valley; two orchards had been planted; and his house of five rooms, not including bathroom and scullery where there was running hot water (my uncle's former occupation as a plumber had been useful), lately finished: the land was carrying nearly as many sheep as it could ever be expected to support. There was in other words, and despite my first impressions (a contradiction which I must in a moment explain), an appearance of settled and civilised pastoral order; the natural order of things, one might have supposed, had been obliged to

yield to intelligent human guidance. But already my uncle had begun to have his doubts. Near the house, on the easier slopes where he had been able to plough, an excellent sole of mixed grasses and clover had been established; but higher up, and away at the back above those clefts, and long before you reached them, the better quality grasses that had grown so lavishly among the litter of fallen burnt trees were beginning to disappear: with a few possible exceptions only the danthonia seemed likely to survive – one of New Zealand's very few natural pastures I fancy, if one doesn't count even coarser growths such as toi-toi and tussock; and even the danthonia was seen to be immediately menaced by biddy-bid and bracken fern – the latter sending up each season an ever more wide-spread forest of coiled shoots, determined and insolent-looking in their strength; and more remotely threatened by the appearance of manuka seedlings, deceptively frail-looking and perhaps even more deceptive by being much less closely packed together as a rule. It wasn't for some years to come that my uncle understood from his own experience the remote meaning of all this: first you had the fern, and if it was left alone it wasn't long before you had the 'second growth', an apparently haphazard collection of tutu wineberry rangiora five-finger and thousand-jacket – besides a dozen other items of small stuff you mightn't be able to name: and then, later on, protected beneath all this wood and fibre, sap and leaf, you discovered the distinct beginnings of the new forest, tiny tender seedlings that promised to become kahikatea totara rimu matai, great trees that could live and flourish hundreds of years after you were dead.

The fern might be checked by crowding it with sheep and cattle when the new season's growth was appearing, but effective crowding would depend upon the subdivision of large paddocks; and the price of fencing wire, to mention just one item, had gone up to an astronomical figure during the years of war. And there remained in any case the problem of the manuka, for the stock an unpalatable item: it was best dealt with by pulling out each piece separately with the human hand, or cutting below ground level if it had grown too large and tough. But the fern and the manuka were only the beginnings of the concrete story. One of the first ominous signs my uncle noticed after the bush had been disposed of was the change in the appearance of the creeks: previously they had been clear, and hadn't seriously flooded after the heaviest kind of rainfall: now a shower would bring them up immediately, and except during the driest spells they would be more or less discoloured. Already there had been a disastrous flood which had washed away the little bridge across the main creek where the road turned into the valley: some of my uncle's fencing had been carried into creeks by the landslides, or buried out of sight yards deep beneath them: sheep and cattle had gone too, to drown or swim, many to disappear. All this had happened two autumns before: I could see for myself the scars left by the landslides, and my uncle took me to see where the creek had scoured out its banks and the soft places of its bed, bringing to light old stumps and logs, some of them immensely large, which had been no part of the bush he had had to deal with: they belonged, he supposed, to a much earlier forest – and one that might well have been destroyed by one or other of the volcanoes that perched with a suggestion of threat high on that nearby airy roof.

What fern manuka and flood had suggested to my uncle's lively and intelligent imagination was something of this kind: namely, that primitive nature in these parts would by no means readily submit to the sort of control which it had been far too easily assumed human energy and labour might impose. And with the years he was to learn a great deal more about the natural order's resourcefulness in hitting back: one might coax the grass to grow on the lifeless and diminishing topsoil with the aid of chemical manures, but almost every year seemed to mark the appearance of some fresh disease among the sheep: comparatively simple complaints such as foot-rot might be dealt with (and in later and more prosperous years quaintly dealt with by providing some of the animals with little rubber boots); but alarming symptoms would appear about which nothing, or next to nothing was known; and quite often a number of the sheep would die. But apart from all these matters there was that other more abstract side to my uncle's farming: his land and stock were mortgaged: fully occupied by his work of transforming the countryside, of trying to bring it closer to the human pattern by making it fruitful in a particular way, he was more or less dictated to and directed by the petty financiers of the neighbouring town of Taumarunui, the local representatives of Big Money, with its centre of power at that time located in the city of London. What did these people care that my uncle had destroyed the bush, and was now having difficulty in creating a stable pasture? All they appeared to be concerned about was that he should pay his interest regularly.

On that first morning when I went outside to look at and be repelled by the bleak silent hills, I did not even faintly understand that my uncle had come such a long way in his first few years: and perhaps it was because I looked mainly at land that belonged to his neighbours, not one of whom had so incredibly managed to cram nearly a hundred years of history into a mere six or seven. One place that didn't quite join on to his own had already been abandoned, never to be taken up again in his lifetime: of those that did join on, one was soon to be abandoned; two would usually be semi-abandoned; another

was maori-owned; and yet one more, about the only one of the entire block that had looked at all attractive to begin with, was never developed to anything like the pitch my uncle achieved – and by his immense lifelong effort maintained. But the result of all this was that one had only to look around to see a truly remarkable variety of country: there was the untouched bush, and on the maori land a very great deal (although it was my uncle's belief that much bush throughout the country had been burned by the maori, perhaps sometimes by accident, long before it was ever seen by the white man); some was still being cut, and where it had been burned you saw land in every stage of reversion if it had been abandoned, or attempted development to stable pasture if it was occupied – although much was always rapidly reverting whether occupied or not, and particularly on the great shady faces which the sun could rarely reach. So although I couldn't know exactly what my uncle's land had originally looked like, any more than he had fore-known what it came to look like after the bush had been cut and burned, I had only to visit his neighbours to see much going on that must certainly have resembled all that I regretted having missed. No doubt I was hoping to experience in actual life the excitement I had got from my vivid imaginings of my brother's stories. Yet I lacked foreknowledge of the human entanglements that actuality might involve me in: it was as though I failed to profit from my experience of the difference between imagining the Te Aroha mountain-top as a sort of private heaven, and actually visiting the same place with a human companion....

The wharf-end windsock takes the day off,

Too apathetic even to raise a cough

Lacking its proper sky-fed food,

Nor is the harbour in the mood

Saltily to lick more coastal blood.

It lies below flat as a doormat,

Quiet as a waiting cat

At mousehole rocks and bides

Its time, waiting for spring tides.

The silly fountain jets and plumes

From the Bay's bottom, endlessly resumes

An appointed pattern to flatten

Waters already flat.

                    I'll say that

It's too idyllically dull, lacks the full

Fretfulness, the sudden umbrella-blaster

Of the bluster of a good sou'wester.

You open the book
& there unfolds a road   its skin is blue, it is summer
the heat   that dances in its hollows turns
into water.   You ride it in the vehicles of strangers:
homesteads & haybarns   dusty yellow sheeptrucks
convoy of soldiers in jungle greens returning

from an exercise   slipping
past their polarized windscreens;
you draw from them splinters   of lives made of words

though you never take your eyes off the mountains.
The mountains   reach out to embrace you
they fold their blue ankles

they give birth to rivers, they
can even crouch like tigers if that's the way you
want them: they are a story you tell

about yourself, a story you are journeying
into, which swallows you.   You leave
the road, then   you honour the logic of ridges

& gorges, of funnels, of slotted
stone chimneys   You startle a huge bird
nesting in the riverbed, climbing on slow

cream & ash coloured wings   & you follow
as it disappears
inland, you tunnel to the spine of the island &

bury yourself   alive, with your possessions, this
curved sky, this whisper of ice-cloud
this magic mountain slamming shut behind you.

It was a monotonous life, but it was very healthy; and one does not much mind anything when one is well. The country was the grandest that can be imagined. How often have I sat on the mountain side and watched the waving downs, with the two white specks of huts in the distance, and the little square of garden behind them; the paddock with a patch of bright green oats above the huts, and the yards and wool-sheds down on the flat below; all seen as through the wrong end of a telescope, so clear and brilliant was the air, or as upon a colossal model or map spread out beneath me. Beyond the downs was a plain, going down to a river of great size, on the farther side of which there were other high mountains, with the winter's snow still not quite melted; up the river, which ran winding in many streams over a bed some two miles broad, I looked upon the second great chain, and could see a narrow gorge where the river retired and was lost. I knew that there was a range still farther back; but except from one place near the very top of my own mountain, no part of it was visible: from this point, however, I saw, whenever there were no clouds, a single snow-clad peak, many miles away, and I should think about as high as any mountain in the world. Never shall I forget the utter loneliness of the prospect – only the little far-away homestead giving sign of human handiwork; – the vastness of mountain and plain, of river and sky; the marvellous atmospheric effects – sometimes black mountains against a white sky, and then again, after cold weather, white mountains against a black sky – sometimes seen through breaks and swirls of cloud – and sometimes, which was best of all, I went up my mountain in a

fog, and then got above the mist; going higher and higher, I would look down upon a sea of whiteness, through which would be thrust innumerable mountain tops that looked like islands.

I am there now, as I write; I fancy that I can see the downs, the huts, the plain, and the river-bed – that torrent pathway of desolation, with its distant roar of waters. Oh, wonderful! wonderful! so lonely and so solemn, with the sad grey clouds above, and no sound save a lost lamb bleating upon the mountain side, as though its little heart were breaking. Then there comes some lean and withered old ewe, with deep gruff voice and unlovely aspect, trotting back from the seductive pasture; now she examines this gully, and now that, and now she stands listening with uplifted head, that she may hear the distant wailing and obey it. Aha! they see, and rush towards each other. Alas! they are both mistaken; the ewe is not the lamb's ewe, they are neither kin nor kind to one another, and part in coldness. Each must cry louder, and wander farther yet; may luck be with them both that they may find their own at night-fall. But this is mere dreaming, and I must proceed.

I could not help speculating upon what might lie farther up the river and behind the second range. I had no money, but if I could only find workable country, I might stock it with borrowed capital, and consider myself a made man. True, the range looked so vast, that there seemed little chance of getting a sufficient road through it or over it; but no one had yet explored it, and it is wonderful how one finds that one can make a path into all sorts of places (and even get a road for

pack-horses), which from a distance appear inaccessible; the river was so great that it must drain an inner tract – at least I thought so; and though every one said it would be madness to attempt taking sheep farther inland, I knew that only three years ago the same cry had been raised against the country which my master's flock was now overrunning. I could not keep these thoughts out of my head as I would rest myself upon the mountain side; they haunted me as I went my daily rounds, and grew upon me from hour to hour, till I resolved that after shearing I would remain in doubt no longer, but saddle my horse, take as much provision with me as I could, and go and see for myself.

The first day we had an easy time, following up the great flats by the river side, which had already been twice burned, so that there was no dense undergrowth to check us, though the ground was often rough, and we had to go a good deal upon the river-bed. Towards nightfall we had made a matter of some five-and-twenty miles, and camped at the point where the river entered upon the gorge.

The weather was delightfully warm, considering that the valley in which we were encamped must have been at least two thousand feet above the level of the sea. The river-bed was here about a mile and a half broad and entirely covered with shingle over which the river ran in many winding channels, looking, when seen from above, like a tangled skein of ribbon, and glistening in the sun. We knew that it was liable to very sudden and heavy freshets; but even had we not known it, we could have seen it by the snags of trees, which must have been carried long distances, and by the mass of vegetable and mineral *débris* which was banked against their lower side, showing that at times the whole river-bed must be covered with a roaring torrent many feet in depth and of ungovernable fury.

At present the river was low, there being but five or six streams, too deep and rapid for even a strong man to ford on foot, but to be crossed safely on horseback. On either side of it there were still a few acres of flat, which grew wider and wider down the river, till they became the large plains on which we looked from my master's hut. Behind us rose the lowest spurs of the second range, leading abruptly to the range itself; and at a distance of half a mile began the gorge, where the river narrowed and became boisterous and terrible. The beauty of the scene cannot be conveyed in language. The one side of the valley was blue with evening shadow, through which loomed forest and precipice, hillside and mountain top; and the other was still brilliant with the sunset gold. The wide and wasteful river with its ceaseless rushing – the beautiful waterbirds too, which abounded upon the islets and were so tame that we could come close up to them – the ineffable purity of the air – the solemn peacefulness of the untrodden region – could there be a more delightful and exhilarating combination?...

For we seem part of this estuary; that is true. I can think of it as an extension of myself. A scatter of houses, pleasingly few, arranged among trees along the shore. And the trees themselves dipping lumpy limbs in the water. Rocks; a stark headland with alien pines. When the tide turns away, there are pools, crabs, dead shells and mud flats. The marvel is that it isn't far from the city. Perhaps a dozen miles. A lost corner, marginally suburban, too rugged for the bulldozer. The treeferns grow lush. And the birds are noisy.

Rangiwai. Translated: waters of the sky. Or Rangiwai of the sylvan slums. Once true. Most parts are perceptibly more immaculate now. A substantial supermarket, satellite shops, a rash of well-groomed homes. In its upper reach. I inhabit the lower; the peninsula. A green and muscular arm of land among mud and mangroves. Still enough untidy dwellings with rusty iron and unpainted weatherboards to keep suburbia at bay. Such evident squalor should be nursed; our time could come....

November 1:
The spring rains have been thunderous. The bush is dank and dourly evergreen again, empty of the kowhai's tint; the vivid drifts of petals have melted from the track. But the pohutukawa is freshening now, with great gusts of young leaf, towards Christmas blooming....

We followed an eroded old timber trail, half hidden under fern, and after steep climbing emerged at last upon the penin-sula road, which would take us homeward; there was a pleasing vista of bright harbour all around, and the distant misty hills towards the mouth were streaking with sunlight. The peninsula road is a single-minded affair, crashing through hump and hollow, and finally and sharply into the sea; it provides a boat-ramp of sorts. There are houses here and there on plots once savagely slashed and incinerated; the habitations grow scantier towards the peninsula's tip. We are retired mostly, we penin-sula-dwellers: from active life, from active love; we pick up our pensions and watch tide and sunset. That is, apart from a boat-builder, a fisherman or two, a sprinkle of launch-loving com-muters, and of course strayed urban refugees of unkempt and questionable occupation such as the Hydes and myself. I sometimes like to think the Maoris who once pottered and paddled about the peninsula, and likely warred over it, may never have had it so good; our wars and wounds are remote now, or private on our properties....

November 27:
Summer again. And true summer, it seems, a month short of the longest day. Thick heat. Manuka and kanuka flowering, frosting those mostly drab trees, and dry clay cracking under-foot, already hugely fissured in places despite the recent rain. The flotsam weed gathers still thicker on the beach, with my compost taking its flavour. Early morning is best for work, before the heat grips, with cool light, hills without haze, and the estuary brittle with beauty. For work appears imperative now. Irene and I make most use of the morning; afternoons

and evenings are left to look after themselves. Another firing has begun. The mullet emerged from the smokehouse tender and sweet; Rose and Tony pronounce them my best ever, and they bring some seasonal piquance to our table. Things could have been less pleasant....

December 6:
My entries begin to thin with the summer, and other things. Other things? The wheel; the kiln. The smoke from our frequent firings makes almost permanent blue mist among the trees. And if not from the kiln, then from the smokehouse; the mullet are running heavy now. Wild waves, in sudden storm last week, gouged the last of the weed from the beach; the sand is clean and white again when we walk there. The old pohutukawa along the shore are pale with tender leaves and buds, freshening for the scarlet bloom of Christmas. My garden, still a place of strong aroma, composted from land and sea, is about to produce. Capsicum and cucumber should arrive well before year's end, with beans and tomatoes following soon. I keep the bugs at bay....

January 4:
First the long antipodean sloth of the season. Now the long antipodean hangover. I observe another year begun. And now try to find the fortnight which has escaped me. The mangroves on the estuary, in this early light, are pale pastures of gold. The house is quiet. It should be some time before anyone wakes. Two women, Irene and sister Beth, currently inhabit the place; I cannot suggest the situation comfortable. But it is a fact. The males in residence, Terror and myself, find refuge here at the desk. The day promises to be another of hot brilliance; perhaps we haven't exhausted the possibilities of picnics on the sand below....

January 17:
The shelves fill slowly. But I am after all working for myself again; Tom Hyde should have sufficient cheques to see him through. I don't ask for account of how the money is spent, so long as it lubricates his enthusiasm to save the estuary from hurt. Insofar as we have conversed lately, he tells me all is quiet on the battle front at the moment; the ecology is safe in the customary rigor mortis of January's heat. Irene finds shelter in the lean-to also. This slack season hasn't stolen the lessons she learned. I like her confidence at the wheel. She even seems an inch or two taller, at times. Imagination, of course; perhaps the confidence too. But I could imagine worse.

The earth smells dry; breezes make arid rattles in the bush; the garden grabs water by the gallon. But the tomatoes are huge, the capsicums burgeoning, and the cucumbers make cool salads for our table. The festive flush of flower along the estuary has faded; the greens grow lacklustre....

February 17:
A full month gone, it seems. We still inhabit the sticky climax of summer. The year still runs in low gear, often drifting in no more than neutral. Perhaps only Irene gives it erratic impetus. The garden is dense with vegetables, aubergines, capsicums, cucumbers, beans; time to bottle and pickle. And I have more fish than I can give away.

In this heat I crave the cool of autumn. Even the fresh and frosty winds of winter. Grey sky and rain bring no relief; the moisture rises humidly from the growth around.

Account for the month? Too painless, perhaps: there is no temptation. I could, this easily, let a year slip past. Or years altogether. No sweat. Even in this heat....

A R D FAIRBURN ◆ *The Estuary*

The wind has died, no motion now
in the summer's sleepy breath. Silver the sea-grass,
the shells and the driftwood, fixed in the moon's vast
    crystal.
Think: long after, when the walls of the small house
have collapsed upon us, each alone,
far gone the earth's invasion
the slow earth bedding and filling the bone,
this water will still be crawling up the estuary,
fingering its way among the channels, licking the stones;
and the floating shells, minute argosies
under the giant moon, still shoreward glide
among the mangroves on the creeping tide.

The noise of gulls comes through the shining darkness
over the dunes and the sea. Now the clouded moon
is warm in her nest of light. The world's a shell
where distant waves are murmuring of a time
beyond this time. *Give me the ghost of your hand:*
unreal, unreal the dunes,
the sea, the mangroves, and the moon's white light,
unreal, beneath our naked feet, the sand.

IAN WEDDE ◆ from *Symmes Hole*

Heberley remembered how the Doctor had sat in that clearing above Anaho – the same easy rounded shoulders... look of ecstasy on his face, as his eyes moved slowly from the high canopies of the big totara, their festoons of orchids up there where the westering light struck down into the clearing, the immense trunk rising without perceptible taper, gripped by tree-thick symbiotic vines – his eyes went up it, and down, and up... in his lap his hands turned palm-up and then clasped each other in an involuntary gesture of awe.

And Heberley watched him survey the place, taking it in stages... he began with the forest floor of ferns, the great mossed-over up-heapings of surface roots... he next took a lateral sweep of the crazy interwoven dangle of supplejack... with an expression of delight and another of those churchy movements of the hands he looked at the ponga tree-ferns, the lovely symmetry of their sectioned trunks and irradiating fronds... the intermediate canopy of young growth, five-finger and lancewoods and young green big-leaved karaka. And then his head tilted slowly back, and he followed the great trunks up again to where they seemed to be toppling forever across the moving clouds which they almost reached... the daft flights of canopy-playing kaka parrots crashing about way up there... dense high clotting of orchids...

And while it was true that Heberley didn't know how to trust the man, he could see that harm wasn't going to come from *him*. And because he'd remembered old Ngarewa telling him, and because he'd begun to feel abashed by the Doctor's silent delight, he flipped out that comment about the stinky lily, and then watched the man's blissful face alter – first a look of doubt, then an expression of sick horror...

'... unmöglich ... das ist ... ach, *nein*... !'

And he saw that Dieffenbach would never again look at the bush with that first expression of ecstasy....

... along the road a trail of Bon Chretien cores, on verges or chucked over fences into blond paddocks, and later just out of reach of surf, all of them loud with wasps drinking the saliva of Kate or Chink, Kate and Chink, as well as sweet pear juice. And somewhere along the way, the empty wine carafe dumped in a forty-four gallon drum rubbish-bin by some beach. A lot of rides, Chink always asking to be let out again. After dark, a cabin at Kaikoura...

That's what Kate's got. She didn't even see the wasps. That's how it is.

Next day Chink shook her awake, pulled off the pink candlewick bedspread and the rayon sheet.

'These Norfolk Pines are the southernmost Norfolk Pines in the world, a tip for The Guide please, ta.'

His shoulders were straight. He was pointing like a dog. He promenaded south under the nitty pines, marginally successful transplants only, even in this temperate enclave: he and Kate were getting into different latitudes, where the 'Philip's Planisphere' (showing the Principle Stars visible for Every Hour in the Year) for lats. 30s-40s which Kate had bought on a whim a week or so ago in Auckland, was going to be unreadable, unless you knew your way around well enough to make the necessary connexions by guesswork. Anyway, had they been able to see the stars in the morning sky, which had a pearly membrane of high cloud stretched across it, and lower down long streamers across the indigo buttresses of the Seaward Kaikouras, they'd have noticed Capricorn rising and chasing Scorpio westwards: Chink being a Capricorn and Kate a

Scorpio, information they've already traded, as a formality. The morning will be spent under sensual Capricorn, while Scorpio slips down behind the barricades in the west. Capricorn rising... by late afternoon Scorpio will be down, Capricorn dropping fast. Come darkness, Kate and Chink will look up at the Pleiades, a tender cluster above the western horizon, and Aldebaran blazing in Taurus. They will leapfrog up the firmament, through Orion to Canis Major, right overhead, just out of range of the scimitar of the Milky Way which, on this night, will sweep in an arc up and through the centre of the sky... Meanwhile the Norfolk Pines stand along the sea marge like burnt-out rockets. At their bases, from desiccated grass, some bright marigolds grow. There's no one else about yet. Towards the western end of the esplanade is an explosion of geraniums... Chink and Kate move on to the beach, a steep ramp of smooth pebbles. The sea bangs the stones around, even though the day is calm and still. Then the beach gives way to rocks. They clamber back up to the road. An oystercatcher, Pinnochio-nose (who's lying?) is fretting down there among the pools, orange beak flashing this way and that against the grey and buff rocks. Other flashes, of light, are breaking through above the cloud streamers against the mountains which Chink and Kate see as they turn to look back across the wide grey bay: there are green pendants on the slopes. A fishing boat is riding at anchor out in the bay. It has a square old-fashioned deck house, high bows. It moves with an odd jerking motion, the bows dipping down the angle of the anchor chain. Ahead of them, past a pale clutter of pumice

along the seashore, they can see the sheds and jetty of the fishing company. Even though the high cloud is beginning to break up, the light is still glaring and low, throwing bright fragments into relief: marigolds, geraniums, the beaks and feet of seabirds, the far-off glass port holes of the fishing boat, green gems at the mountains' throats... A sudden ricochet of light off the tin roof of the fishery sends a shatter of reflections among the windows of cars around the buildings. Then the cloudy retina closes again... the scene remains as though photographed: foreshortened, clear, birds hung in still air... and something has happened to your eyes: having trapped that detonation of light they stare back past white cataracts... In the doorway of Virgo Fisheries Ltd lolls a man with such an eye, nacreous disc at its centre. Behind him fish are slapped on slabs... white rubber aprons and smears of blood... the quick flicking of knives... while a transistor radio emits the squawks of a commercial breakfast programme.

'Gidday.'

'How are ya.'

The man flicks his cigarette butt out on the asphalt and turns back inside.

Gulls fight over fish-heads floating below some concrete steps where the high tide mark shows at a greeny line of slime and weed. There are triangular orange trickles of oxide below iron rings in the concrete pier. Some rowboats have been pulled up on to the dock. Cloudy rainwater and fish-scales wash over the base boards.

The cloud is really lifting now, the membrane getting thinner, tearing here and there. The atmosphere is heavy. There is no sea wind. In the dusty stands of weed along the gravel road where Kate and Chink are walking the insects are starting up: 'Wit wit wit'. Under this is a persistent harsh continuo: the vibrations seem to strike at the *inside* of some

deep part of their ears. The sea now resembles molten lead. Two grey herons cast perfect reflections on slick sand. Chink and Kate walk past a fishing boat beached for refitting. It's being painted bright yellow. Lower down are uncompleted brush strokes of red lead. Along the side of the road is a dry waste of thistle and tussock, grey with pumice dust.

They come to a flat moonscape of rock where the road ends. Here the planes and surfaces are smooth and extend on all sides with shallow catchments of water which reflect light. The rock, wrinkled in soft folds like the skin of some great beast, has a silvery patina. Limpets cling to this skin like warts. Chink and Kate walk across it, past bladderweed and kelp embracing smooth white stones. The beast-skin gives way to such stones, these to a clanking volcanic rubble and a dark sea marge where lizards flick and shuffle into shadow. The lizards seem oily, yet they move with dry precision: *flick, flick,* like their tongues. In the dark crannies where the sea is washing the kelp glistens as though oily... stirring in the shallows and clefts of rock.

Then the grey is swept away by sunlight. The cloud membrane has torn right across. High puffs of cirrus trot over blue sky. Heat bounces off the rock. Bumblebees stagger by, inept formations of shags make it to shit-splattered rocks where they spread their wings to the sun. Thistle, low thorn bushes and flax begin cracking and popping with heat.

Her eyes have gone nacreous, they're shining blindly with tears like the mother-of-pearl eyes of a watchful guardian, her glass cage of memory is jangling, the Wedding Guest opposite her is shaking her head and whispering, 'Oh fuck, oh fuck...'.

That distance! She's really feeling it... on that barbaric rind of coast: Chink's scale, the spaces he's hooked on: nothing less than that transparent blue distance, into which the mind pours out, like an estuary into the sea...

'Can I come with you?' She senses some kind of progression from her Badedas bath to that Pacific skyline! Now, there's a weird one! So all at once she's laughing and laughing. She's *free...*

At this point Chink has stopped. A deep sound comes from low in his chest.

'What is it?' Like a child deep into some game, she's ready to believe anything.

He's staring ahead, past a pagoda-shaped rock formation on the edge of a stagnant inlet. Beyond this murky water is a small hillock. It's chalky, shaped like a shoulder blade, a dry scuff of tussock at its base, its upper edge scalloped sharp by wind. Beyond it the coast, precipitous and darkened with cloud above the ranges, recedes into the heat haze, a bare escarpment shining here and there where sunlight breaks through. Above the cloudy ranges the sky is a bleached-out blue, and below, where the deeper colours of the sea show among brown and white ribs and snags of rock, there's a flickering show of light, like thousands of jostling candles in some temple or procession.

'Hey, what is it?'

They skirt around the shoulder blade. Once their ears have got used to the sound of the waves and have dismissed it, the silence is trance-like. Not even birds.

'What is it, where are we gong?'

She inhales a hot waft of something rank and feral, so sudden it shocks her, like a loud clap of noise by her ear. Birds scream upwards from the jagged rock formation ahead: terns and blackbacks, red insides of gaping beaks.

'Ah the darlings, the darlings!' Chink has stopped again, his face broken by a helpless grin of such release as she's only seen when he's making love... Thinking he means the birds she looks up but he seizes her head and jerks it down, pointing her gaze at the gnarled confusion of rocks ahead.

And there they are: the seals, at ease on the jagged rocks: lithe plump flanks... eyes large and dark and lovely, long lashed, tranquil pools... yawning with satisfaction, a flipper scratching at buff pelt... tender muzzles. Kate can see them everywhere, lolling on their stomachs or sides, or else propped up, small heads in the air, catching the sun and the breeze.

Some of those near-at-hand heave themselves in fright to the sea, and slide in. At once their grace is miraculous: shrugging off gravity like water over their shoulders, they turn to look back, sleek heads snouting up, huffing sea from their nostrils, and then dive away again, unthreatened, corkscrewing sideways with flippers slapping the surface of the water, browsing through dark kelp and bladderweed along the sides of the rocks, through the surge and backsuck of the swell, across ripcurrents at the mouths of deep clefts, and from time to time driving on their tails up out of the water for long enough to shake a spray of sea from their pelts....

PATRICIA GRACE ◆ from *Waiariki*

There were three different places where we went for kai moana. The first, about a mile round the beach, called Huapapa, was a place of small lagoons and rock pools. The rocks here were large and flat and extended well out into the sea. This was a good place for kina and paua and pupu. We would ride the horses out as far as we could and tether them to a rock. They would stand there in the sun and go to sleep. To get kina we would go out to where the small waves were breaking, in water about knee deep. We'd peer into the water, turning the flat stones over, and it wouldn't take long to fill a sugar-bag with kina. The paua were there too, as well as in the rock pools further towards shore. The younger children, who were not old enough to stand in the deeper water and not strong enough to turn the big rocks for paua and kina, would look about in the rock pools for pupu, each one of them hoping to find the biggest and the best.

The next place, Karekare, further round the beach, was also a good place for shellfish, but the reason we liked to go there was that there was a small lagoon with a narrow inlet, which was completely cut off from the sea at low tide. Often at low tide there were fish trapped there in the lagoon. And we

children would all stand around the edge of the lagoon and throw rocks at the fish.

'Ana! Ana!' we'd yell.

'Patua! Patua!' hurling the stones into the water. And usually there would be at least one fish floating belly up in the lagoon by the time we'd finished. Whoever jumped in first and grabbed it would keep it and take it home....

The other place, Waiariki, is very special to me. Special because it carries my name which is a very old name and belonged to my grandfather and to others before him as well. It is a gentle quiet place where the lagoons are always clear and the brown rocks stand bright and sharp against the sky. This was a good place for crayfish and agar. Mum was the one who usually went diving for crayfish, ruku koura. She would walk out into the sea fully clothed and lean down into the water, reaching into the rock holes and under the shelves of rock for the koura. Sometimes she would completely submerge, and sometimes we would see just a little bit of face where her mouth was, sitting on top of the sea....

ALLEN CURNOW ◆ *You Will Know When You Get There*

Nobody comes up from the sea as late as this
in the day and the season, and nobody else goes down

the last steep kilometre, wet-metalled where
a shower passed shredding the light which keeps

pouring out of its tank in the sky, through summits,
trees, vapours thickening and thinning. Too

credibly by half celestial, the dammed
reservoir up there keeps emptying while the light lasts

over the sea, where it 'gathers the gold against
it'. The light is bits of crushed rock randomly

glinting underfoot, wetted by the short
shower, and down you go and so in its way does

the sun which gets there first. Boys, two of them,
turn campfirelit faces, a hesitancy to speak

is a hesitancy of the earth rolling back and away
behind this man going down to the sea with a bag

to pick mussels, having an arrangement with the tide,
the ocean to be shallowed three point seven metres,

one hour's light to be left and there's the excrescent
moon sponging off the last of it. A door

slams, a heavy wave, a door, the sea-floor shudders.
Down you go alone, so late, into the surge-black fissure.

A Pattern of Voices

I Kapiti   An island near Cook Strait once the stronghold of Te Raupahara (1770-1849)

This island is alive with ghosts.
Tonight every leaf is an ear
attuned to your heartbeat,
every stick a spear
gripped by a crouching figure...
Their eyes glint
on the moonlit hillsides,
and their oiled bodies
bending towards you in their hundreds
gleam like flax...
Listen!
What is that sound
like the sound of waves on the rocks?
But there is no wind —
even the sea is asleep.
Listen!
The sea begins to wake in its wide bed
and whispers of war.
A thousand paddles shatter
the drowning moon,
a bridge of war canoes
spans the troubled sea
between Kapiti and the mainland...
It is no use.

Numbers cannot save you.
Nothing can save you now
but your swift paddles.
Te Rauparaha is a god

and Kapiti is his backbone.
Even the moon is his ally.

Men of the mainland,
be counselled and turn back.
Your streams are full of eels
and your valleys throb with pigeons
that are yours for the taking...
What tempted you to Kapiti?
Your wives are hot and willing
and will approve far more
than the scowling Ngati Toa
the adroitness of your stick play...
Aue! It is too late.
Already steam rises from your heads
as from an oven,
and the maddened Rangihaeata
roasts alive his suppliant kinsman
Rangimairehau...
Enough — it is done!
Mothers, put on the leaves of mourning —
wail for your sons.
Weep, widows,
slash your foreheads.
Howl, depleted tribes,
for your dishonoured manhood
whose bones lie scattered
on the shores of Kapiti.

We drove to Woodside Glen on the Taieri Plain where a stream fell down from Maungatua among huge mossed rocks beneath the beeches; to Whare Flat, a narrow valley on the far side of Flagstaff, the hill behind Dunedin, where a quieter stream rambled over the stones and changed to clear glass beside a bluff in the shelter of the warm bushed ridges, and in spring the old kowhai trees were hung with heavy dark-gold flowers. During school holidays, a family party sometimes rented the school house there, in order to explore the country round, from Chalky and Swampy up to Mt Allan and the Silver Peaks.

But I think I always preferred the sea to the hills, whether at the northern beaches or those of Otago Peninsula. From an early excursion I remember our stopping as we drove round the sharp bends of the rocky upper Peninsula road, behind Peggy's Hill, to pick everlasting daisies. Grandmother probably first told me their name, so that they came to seem her flowers, as if their leaves and petals went naturally with the ivory and dry cool green of her tussore silk veils and parasols. They grew profusely on the banks there, crawled over stones, hung down in a rough curtain half concealing bare clay scars. Their dry silver-white petals enclosed an eye of clear honey or pale lime green like a cat's, the dark green leaves, silver beneath, grew from much-jointed stems softly furred with silver, and in shrivelling turned pale brown. I pressed everlastings in books, as Grandmother and my aunts did, picked them for vases, decorated straw hats with them. Later I thought of them as my chosen flower of all the natives, as exquisite as they were common and unpretending; 'the honey eyes of the everlastings' was a phrase I stored up for years, waiting for the right poem to put it in.

Our special beaches on the Peninsula were Little Papanui near Cape Saunders lighthouse, and Pipikariti, some miles further towards the Otago Heads. Nearly always we had them to ourselves; it was unusual to meet other people, and we came to think of them as our own ground. At Pipikariti and other beaches Grandfather searched the sands methodically, drawing his walking stick behind him to mark where he had gone, for what we children called Maori curios – adzes, fish-hooks of bone and shell, flint knives, drills, stone sinkers, greenstone and whale's tooth pendants. The winds were constantly at work on those beaches shifting the sands about, so that buried objects were always being uncovered, and finds continued to be made for many years. I sometimes followed Grandfather's example, and trod the surface of the sand poking among the fragments of shell, fish and animal and bird bone, obsidian, the stones and wood, that marked sites once occupied. But unless I made a lucky find I was soon ready to give up; I did not learn Grandfather's method. When I was, once, unusually lucky, and came on a good greenstone pendant, Grandfather appropriated it for his collection or for the Museum; sensibly, no doubt, since it was too fine a piece to be left in my capricious possession.

The rough poor land above broke down to Pipikariti beach in irregular low winding cliffs, about the reddish faces of which grew straggling ngaio trees and kowhais and occasional elder bushes; thick growths of muehlenbeckia creeper here and

there formed small cave shelters against the rock; below, grassy or swampy flats lay between the cliffs and the sandhills, overgrown in places with nearly impenetrable thickets of gorse or lupin. On the slopes above stood a dilapidated Maori cottage where we might see a few children, sometimes with a cow or a rather sorry horse; but if the children ever came near I do not remember that we played with them or even exchanged words. Ours was usually a sizable party, so that we had ample company; later anyway it often included other children, Eunoe, or John and Biddy Laing, between whose family and ours there had been a long friendship, and perhaps school friends as well. We boiled the billy and lunched near the cliffs, where there was wood and may have been water – to some beaches we had to take water with us. In hot weather we bathed. Some of the party explored the edges of the beach and the cliffs; at Little Papanui if not at Pipikariti penguins and seals were sometimes to be found; at the sea's edge and along the tide-marks we gathered shells and seaweed to wonder at and take home at the end of the day. Sun and sand and a salty tang of breeze to burn our faces, the scents of manuka and lupin and wood fires in the open air, tea delicately smoked from black crusted billies – these made part of family life.

I grew to know most of the country about Dunedin, in all its variousness. It impressed itself on me so strongly that it seemed to accompany me always, becoming an interior landscape of my mind or imagination, unchanging, archetypal, the setting of what I read about as well as of all the life of the present. The shapes, textures, scents, sounds of all its landscapes grew into me and grew with me.

Near the horse-trough on Flagstaff where the road dips down to Whare Flat, one of our favourite spots for boiling the billy, I used to look inland across tussock declivities and bush valleys and smoke-blue ridges that led eye and imagination on into airy distances not at all diminished because they contained real places named and mapped; in their infinite possibility dream and reality became one. Or I looked south from the hills on blue days along the coast to Brighton and Taieri Mouth and to that long arm lying far out to sea at the end of which lay The Nuggets, sea and shore and islands floating together in the light haze of the air, in the sound of waves that I imagined but could not catch. Later, I knew that sea as the great southern ocean rolling for monotonous hundreds of miles round the bottom of the world, and frozen at last in the floes and bergs of the Antarctic and the deathly whiteness of the last silent lifeless continent. A grey cold sea for much of the year, it beat blindly all along the stubborn coast, shaking, undermining, wearing away, attacking the very roots of the land; on still nights after storm I could hear it, low and far off, muttering as it flung in desperation up the empty beaches. In the sea you feel and hear and watch the earth's pulse; winds come out of space, etherial breath, but ocean tides are the very breathing of earth itself....

The cold wind encouraged us to move quickly where possible, keeping on the sheltered Linda side of the ridge. The morning light increased our confidence; we relaxed and climbed more fluently as our bodies, prodded by necessity, adjusted to the cold, brown rock around us. Already the peaks of Dampier, Hicks and the Navigator Range lay below, and beyond, still separated from the dawn by the mountain heights, the bush and coastal plain of Westland lay in a deep, blue light which merged them with the ocean. Only a line of liquid white marked the transition from forest to sea-water. It was an immense world of mountain, forest, cloud and ocean, made real to us by a momentary perception: as the sun rose on the other side of Mount Cook it cast the mountain's shadow over our heads, far, far out over the ocean, a vast, transparent form that severed the whiteness of the morning sky as it reached for the horizon. Lost in its sombre, impalpable mass, we cast no shadow at all.

To keep the climb demanding we went straight up the pleasant steepness of the first step in the ridge. Where the angle eased we reached the sun, soothing and reassuring, then on up the crest of the ridge with the sunlit Linda Glacier below out left, and on the right the still beshadowed Hooker. At the foot of the final step Bruce took over the lead. He climbed up the wall on big, solid flakes until he was below an evil-looking overhang of brittle rock; then he traversed right, onto a face, only to come up against a blank wall separating us from the steep gully by which the normal route bypasses the step. To reach the gully required a pendulum on the rope, a manoeuvre which seemed more complicated than it should have and which stretched us across the wall like mentally-deficient flies caught in a web. To excuse our clumsiness and the time frittered away, we reminded ourselves that, after all, this was only the first real climb of the season.

But even on the normal route we made slow progress. The highest rocks were badly iced, forcing us at one point to pull ourselves up on an ice screw and, elsewhere, to clear the rock of the huge ice feathers that had been deposited by storms and bristled in the direction of the wind. Then we heaved ourselves onto the last ledge and abruptly the rock ended: above rose the ice-cap, glittering green and hard under its thin dusting of snow, but from this side offering a short, gentle climb to the summit. Using crampons it took no time at all. Tired, relieved at having to climb no further, we sat down in the snow on the sheltered side of the peak to rest.

The summit of New Zealand; a gentle dome of snow at the junction of a complex of ridges that stands against the clouds; the climax of the mountain range which straddles the Roaring Forties and deflects the winds from their course around the world. All around us mountain faces fell into the void. To the west, close enough below us to distinguish the lines of surf breaking on the beach, lay the Tasman Sea, while to the east, indistinguishable in a fusion of plain and cloud and haze, the Pacific Ocean rose and fell upon the shore. We were so much higher that even the nearby peaks appeared to have shrunk to an indifferent height. Immediately below was rocky Dampier; then the hanging glacier of Vancouver; Malaspina; the needles of Drake and Magellan, overshadowed by the symmetrical beauty of Tasman, with the satellite peak of Torres behind; and in the background the lesser peaks of the Navigator Range descending towards the forest and rivers of Westland. To the left of Dampier rose the compact dome of Hicks crowned with blue ice cliffs; and beyond that La Perouse, that giant mountain hub which spins off ice-falls and ridges in all directions.

Would those great navigators have been horrified at the thought of being commemorated in useless lumps of rock and ice raised at the edge of nowhere? I doubt it. Surely they had humanity enough to see the correctness of the association, the appropriateness of linking mountain grandeur with the names of men who devoted themselves to attaining something that lay beyond social dictates or personal gain, who were prepared to risk personal safety, not from moral compulsion or for profit, but in order to make existence a fuller, more complete affair, and who chose to move into the dimension of growth rather than stagnate in the mire of inheritance.

It is incredible that Captain Cook should sail to his death at Kealakekua Bay in order to support the family he rarely saw, or to serve the country that gave him little except new sailing orders whenever he returned. He could not have sailed in expectations of reward. If he had, Tasman would have been able to disillusion him. After the epic voyage on which he circumnavigated the Australian continent and, in the shadow of the Southern Alps, sailed up the West Coast of New Zealand, losing several crew members to hungry Maoris en route, Tasman was coldly received by his employers, who were most displeased that he should be so wasteful of East India Company money and possessions as to return to Java, with empty holds. No, the navigators undertook their voyages because to sail was to be free.

That realm of action which goes beyond self-interest and material need is what we solemnise with the name of culture: culture is what people do because they want to rather than because they must; its actions are to be understood in their own terms rather than the assumption that they must lead somewhere or produce a tangible result. If you like: culture is where what is commonly called causality breaks down. But although it is gratuitous and superfluous, it is not random or destructive. Culture is rooted in natural and social order.

Voyaging is one kind of exploration of reality, one type of creativity which requires its own particular skills and abilities. Science is another; and from where we were sitting on Mount Cook – passing around biscuits and sardines, getting cold behinds – we could see the peaks named after those who chose to pursue science: Lendenfeld's fluted ice showed to the right of Tasman, the serrated skyline of Haast behind it, and Haidinger's broad mass sending its glaciers down to the Tasman Valley floor; at the head of the Tasman Glacier the Main Divide pivoted around Elie de Beaumont, while the rocky peaks of Darwin, Haeckel and Malte Brun lined the far side of the glacier, with the crest of the Liebig Range disappearing behind them to the east....

SAM HUNT ◆ *A White Gentian*

Remember Ruapehu,
that mountain, six months ago?
You sat in an alpine hut
sketching scoria, red
rusted outcrops in the snow.

I climbed some southern peak
and made up the sort of song
men climbing mountains sing:
how, no longer your lover,
I knew it was over.

I thought I'd try out my song
when I returned that evening
as though there were nothing wrong.
Instead I brought a flower down
Smelling of the mountain.

WITI IHIMAERA ◆ from *Tangi*

Waituhi... It is the place of the heart. A Maori village a few miles from Gisborne. There are no shops, no reason at all for Waituhi to be here except that this is the hearth of the Whanau A Kai. This is their home and here they live.

A road runs through the whanau and the houses are strung like beads along the road. Some of the houses are very old, with paint peeling from the boards and rusting corrugated roofs. Others are State houses, shining and new. Some are just tin shacks, with newspaper and pictures from magazines as wallpaper. Dirt tracks lead from the road and along them live others of my family. Small wooden houses dot the fields. Some are hidden in tall waving maize. Others are clustered about with fruit trees and willows. On one side of Waituhi are the hills, pushing small spurs down toward the village. Upon them graze cattle and sheep. On the other side, the flat land rolls away to the river. The river has changed its course across this country many times. During the winter, it becomes swollen with silted water. But it does not overflow across the land as it once used to because not long ago, men came to control the river and created a new course for the ravaging water. From the road, you can still see the loops and bends of the old river bed, now green with pasture. This river, for me, is like that river which once flowed through Eden. And this place, Waituhi, is my Eden.

Just as there was a gateway to Eden, so also is there a gate to Waituhi. The road curves round a small hill where an old colonial home now stands. Once, there used to be a Maori stockade upon that hill. You can still see the terraces where the tall wooden fences used to be. Every day, returning from school in Gisborne, the bus passed by the hill. Eagerly, I would peer forward. The hill would slide past. The road would curve round it. There, in front, would be Waituhi. A small place.

At one bend, houses cluster near an old church. Dad and I would often walk along the road, past these houses. If we met anybody we would stop and talk. Sometimes, somebody would wave to us and we'd wave back. If it was twilight, always somewhere we'd hear a guitar being strummed. This was the Whanau A Kai. This was home.

On another bend in the road, is the meeting house, the house of the whanau. Rongopai. It is set near the side of a hill. Beside the meeting house is a tin cookhouse. Behind, there are fields, some covered with gorse. Rongopai. The meeting house of the Whanau A Kai.

People often pass by in their cars and never see Rongopai. For them perhaps, it is just another meeting house, decaying in the wind. But for me, Rongopai is like my father. Home. The place of the heart. The centre of my universe. And Dad would often take me there. He would unlatch the gate and we would stand before it, silent a moment. I would see the roof, sloping upward to the painted koruru at the apex and it would look as if it was holding up the sky. I would see the paint peeling from the panels of the maihi, the boards extending like arms from the koruru, to welcome me. Inside the porch, I would glimpse swirling kowhaiwhai designs and other painted decorations. This was the meeting house of my tupuna. And it was my meeting house too.

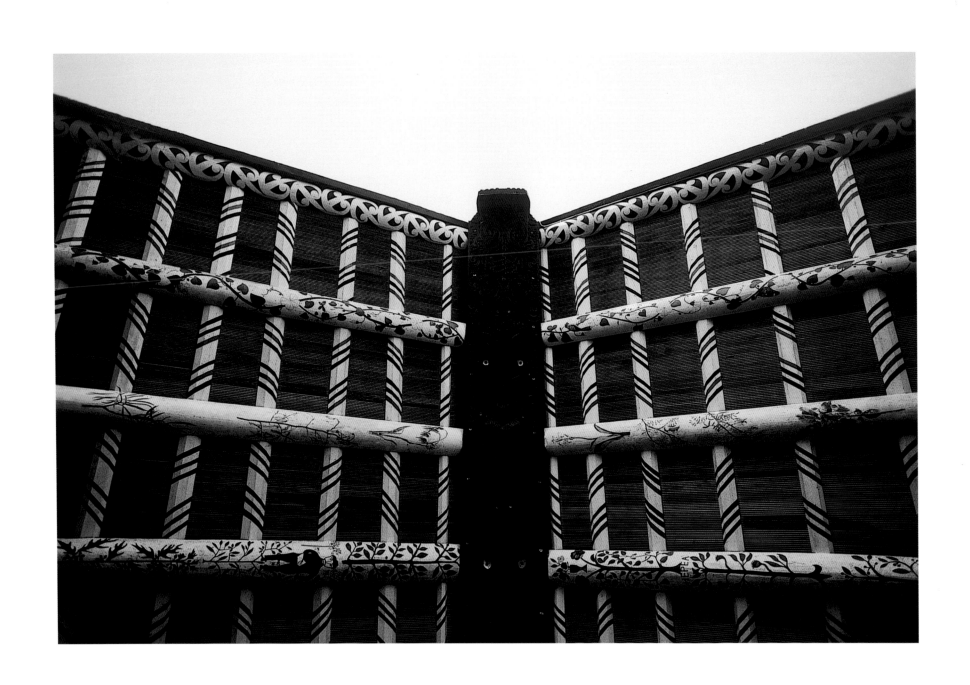

103

It was built for Te Kooti, Dad told me. That was long ago, even before Dad's time. The work was carried out by the young men, who painted it with bright swirling colours. It was one of the very few painted meeting houses remaining and still beautiful to look upon, despite the decay brought by wind, rain and sun. But when it was finished, the elders came and were shocked at what they saw. The young men, in decorating the house, had departed from the traditional designs. The old reverence and dignity had gone. In its place, the young men had blended both Maori and Pakeha art and scenes of life together. For the elders, this was not right. But you told me, Dad, that perhaps even then, the young men had seen that the old life was ending. And this meeting house for you, was a symbol of the twilight years of the Maori. As it had been foretold, so it had come to pass... the shadow behind the tattooed face had come to claim the world.

Kei muri i te awe kapara he tangata ke,
mana te ao, he ma.
Shadowed behind the tattooed face
a stranger stands, he who owns the earth,
and he is white...

You said this with sadness, e pa, the very first time we visited Rongopai. With resignation, you told me that everything in this world decays and falls. I did not understand. Then you stepped onto the porch, unlocked the door and beckoned me inside. As I followed you, it seemed as if I was entering another world. There was no other light except that which streamed through the open door.

I gasped, e pa, at the sight of the house. I was filled with wonder. The panels were like tall trees, elaborately decorated, extending along both walls like a pathway into a forest. Some of the panels were painted with Maori designs and some with sinuous twining plants, like vines curling upward to the roof. Fantastic birds flew through that timeless forest and fruits and flowers seemed to open crimson petals to the light. People climbed among the branches and glittering creatures of another world soared upward to the rafters.

As I followed you into Rongopai, that world reached outward to enclose me. The floor was dirt and it seemed as if the panels were living trees, taking root there. Here was where my tupuna, my ancestors lived. You pointed them out to me, e pa, and showed me how the young men had changed tradition. On one panel, was an ancestor who wore in his hair not the royal huia feather but a Scotch thistle. On another, a young woman stood, timeless in a Pakeha gown, holding a rose to her lips. Strange animals appeared from amid the painted foliage. At a third panel, I knelt down to take a closer look at two men sparring in a boxing match. And there, on a fourth, horses gleamed as they lifted their hooves in a never- ending race. Right at the end of the building, figures reached out of the darkness to brandish taiaha and mere at me.

I held you tightly then, e pa. You laughed and told me not to be afraid. These were my people and this was my meeting house. This house and these people were glad that I had come, you said. I listened and it seemed as if I heard laughter, glittering like a waterfall in my ears... and I was not afraid.

And I looked up at the roof, my eyes following the glistening creatures as they slithered amid the stars of that woven sky.

We stayed there for a long time, e pa. I felt the heart beating in that house. You spread your arms and told me that all this was why the elders had prophesied that Te Kooti would never enter Rongopai. They made it tapu. Te Kooti never did visit Waituhi.

Then we left Rongopai. I watched as you closed the door.

The light narrowed within the house and the forest plunged into darkness.

We turned and walked away. I looked back.

E pa, Rongopai, it was holding up the sky....

You could see all Waituhi from that hill. The road curving away and the houses of the whanau. And far away on the outskirts, was our farm and the farmhouse. Even from the hill, you could make out the gabled eaves and the verandah. Often I would go to the hill, just to sit and be content. This was my world, and the surrounding hills defined its limits. In winter, the mist cascaded down the hills or sleets of rain covered Waituhi with a gray haze. In summer, it seemed that my world extended as the hills receded into the sky. Spring brought green fields and crops of maize and the orchards grew ripe with fruit. Autumn was the season of falling leaves. But no matter what season, it seemed to me that Waituhi remained unchanged. Sometimes, when the sun was going down, the hills would be set alight with a coronet of fire. At such times, I would look at the lights of Waituhi and be calm. Far away, I would see the lamplight gleaming from our own house, and know I was not alone. And always, during the closing night, as I walked from the hill back home, there would be the sound of a guitar and a voice to sing my loneliness away.

Me, he manurere, aue,
Kua rere tito, moenga
Ki te awhi toti, nana
Aue, aue, e te tota huri mai...

The carriage fills with the strains of the girl as she strums idly on her guitar and sings quietly to herself. The train rocks and sways, as if to the rhythm of her song. This girl, she is recalling her own life with her Nanny. Her song also fills me with more memories, taunting and playful, of Waituhi my home. Some of the images are wistful and magical and as fleeting as the wind....

Waituhi is family. The whanau is my home. The love and affection they hold for each other are the ridgepoles of my heart. The sharing and enjoying of each other are the rafters. And within those walls and roof, my heart is shared with my whanau, so closely intertwined, that even now, I pine for home.

Taku manawa, a ratou manawa.

My heart is their heart. And their heart is mine. I am their father, son and friend. They too, are my mothers, fathers, sons and friends. Away from them. I feel lost. Away from the heart I am lonely. But soon I will return. This train takes me further away from Waituhi. I will walk the streets of Wellington and I will be sad. Then I will return home, still lonely, because Dad has gone from me. Mere will be waiting for me as she was the night I returned home to farewell my father.

Kua mate taku papa....

JANET FRAME ◆ from *Living in the Maniototo*

Blenheim is a suburb of Auckland. It is a special suburb in that, although it has many of the highly prized and priced views, it is not bordered by ocean and it lies between the more popular holiday beaches and the road to the northern coastal playgrounds of Auckland city. If you, a stranger, stay in Blenheim, you stay in a motel on your way to your "real" destination. If you live there, you either live in a town house or a home unit or a family house no older than twenty-five, and your streets are named after British lords and their country seats, and battles of wars recent and long ago.

If the creation of Blenheim out of forest land had been a natural event in geological time using the slow force of wind, wave, and sun, it would have taken 250 million years, and the lives of the earliest inhabitants would burn today as coal burns to light the memory of the earliest trees in a primeval forest, lighting and warming with the dreams of the past. But the life of Blenheim has not happened that way. It's a violent suburb. The children are restless, with a sense of loss, as if they had truly been children of the native forest which, like a father, has abandoned them by dying. Blenheim has a higher proportion of suicides than the marine suburbs; more robberies, car conversions, civil and supreme court cases, more arson, bounced checks. Yet it also has the skilled workers, the plumbers, carpenters, potters, mechanics, french polishers. It has dancers, a taxidermist, florists, a ventriloquist (Violet Pansy Proudlock!). And from recent years there has been the ghost of the famous poet who collapsed in the street and died in the house of Violet Pansy Proudlock. ("I took him in," she said,

"and put him on my sofa beside my talking stick and my pocket head and he died there, and I covered his face with Iceland poppies.")

And now they say that whenever a black fantail appears at your back door, it brings the ghost of the poet to you. Perhaps you may feed the fantail and then watch it flutter and dance away to the Hastings Domain where all that is left of the native forest is allowed to grow among the macrocarpa trees and the pampas grass and the half-buried car-bodies.

A city is proud to have a poet: Blenheim is proud to have the little black fantail.

The havoc of a concentrated 250 million years of the human touch lies also on the northeastern outskirts of Blenheim, in the industrial estate known as Kaka Valley with its many factories, and timber, and concrete works; and because if you take part, however remotely, in destruction, you also take pleasure in recreating what you have destroyed, there are many plant nurseries in Kaka Valley where you may buy all the native shrubs and trees as well as the more quickly growing silver dollar gum, and casuarina, and sweet pea, which will screen your house from the neighbors when you and they play stereos, fight, make love, write dud checks, or commit suicide.

Blenheim. The disinherited suburb-city where the largest, most impressive building is not a cathedral, a community hall, concert hall or theater, but a shopping mall planned by those who believe that the commercial architecture of North America is suitable for Blenheim: built for a climate of blizzards, intense heat, meagre daylight filtered through smog; for

a city where the stars and the sun and the sky are no longer part of the human view. Heavenfield Mall at the top of Heavenfield Street, overlooking the harbor and its islands that are themselves shapes of sunlight, is a huge windowless pretence, as much an insinuation of Elsewhere as its own name or that of the city or of the restaurant, Manhattan, at its entrance. In Heavenfield Mall (known as Heavenfield City) during the school holidays there are concerts, games, circus acts, giant raffles for the children while the parents buy buy buy for cash or credit their furniture, electrical appliances, food, a variety of services—international flower delivery, hairdressing, dental and medical care. A consumer's paradise enhanced, you will notice, by the aviary on the second floor where canaries and lovebirds sing, and fly in flashes of blue and yellow, an arrogant costly restoration and reminder, however, of the lost noise of the sun.

What is Blenheim? I used to see market researchers writing down a citizen's preference for this or that brand of bedhead, mattress, house paint; social researchers exploring the emotional consumption by asking intimate questions from door to door; while every week in the free local newspaper, the *Blenheim Advertiser*, an editor or minister or magistrate delivered a condemning judgment about Blenheim and its inhabitants. For a young new suburb named after a "famous victory," it is a place of defeat and unhappiness, caught in the historic confusion of many battles, full of "shocking sights" where the flower gardens hide the human skulls, where the hammers hammer and the saws saw as the cardboard home units with their aluminum joinery, summit stone fireplaces, Wunda Kitchens, take shape in the streets of unimaginable death — El Alamein Road, Corrunna Crescent, Malplaquet Place, Alexander Avenue, Northumbria Drive, Hohenlinden Avenue "Inviting fires of death to light the darkness of her scenery," Lucknow Place, Bannockburn Road, Maldon Square (a small square at the top of the hill near Heavenfield City, composed of fashionable townhouses with floor-to-ceiling windows and glass front doors frosted with butterflies or with deer-shapes against snowy mountains and pine trees). Yet for all the historic confusion and insinuation, and the pride in the streets of the famous generals and the one street dedicated to a famous footballer, and the one to a ballet dancer who "made good" in another country, and the memories, halfway up Heavenfield Road, in Peach Place and Apple Road, once the site of orchards and pumpkin farms, the sense of loss cannot be masked, even if it is clearly revealed only in the older generation that lives in the earliest houses that once were baches and still have the old corrugated iron tank at the back of the house, and the picket-doored dunny at the end of the garden, and the flowers that you can't buy — granny's bonnets and violets—though, mind you, the seasons in Auckland are not as tuned to many of the spring flowers, they're haphazard seasons with summer the supreme commander. Spring is personal—your peach tree and mine do not blossom at the same time; our freesias and daffodils live in different seasons. This undisciplined autonomy of vegetation is reflected in the uncontrolled growth of the city and the suburbs, and is shown in the people as a freedom of mood and impulse which would horrify the souls of many South Islanders restricted by their absolute boundaries of frost....

KIRSTY GUNN ◆ from *Rain*

Even in dry summer, water. That part of the country was a carved-out bowl for rivers running to it, rain. My father could predict the floods and freak storms in their thick cloud colours, yellow for thunder, indigo for lightning. It was geography, he said, the cold plunging depth of a volcanic lake and the warm air banked up around the mountains. Marriage in the way they attracted, in the way water banked up and had to break. We swam in water that changed colour by the weather. See-through for the hot days in the shallows, pale chiffon-blue deeper, dark underskirts beneath. Other times, when close storms held the lake still as black glass, you could believe it might bruise you... Then the wind blew up and the whole surface shattered and cut into a million shining bits, exposing the jelly insides of the water within, cobalt, silken.

So much water. Miles of it under you, washing through underwater caves, one shelf of water tipping over into another, vast secret lakes, a whole world of water beneath, prehistoric. It was hundreds of miles of past and future washing through itself in endless, moonless tides. Water, water, all water. Of course our mark upon it, our frail kicking... Of course it could have been no more than leaves scattered across the surface. So much water, you can't change it. You can imagine other things you could have done, if you want, rack over in your mind details, events, names of people and their ages... But does any of this give you more than what you started out with?

The water has them, those people you pretend were your life. It has you. It's water's pulse beating in your wrist now. You know it too. The lake, she's your lovely body now, with all her openings. Close your eyes, she's still there. Some days the surface of water is pulled over like satin, others it's rumpled and bony. There's your memory. Pure images of tide and depth and the colour of the water... These are things you can still use. Who you were, who you are now, your people... They're drowned in her. All the rest is water.

I remember how, long ago, my little brother and I used to go out into the summer rain. We were disappearing or returning, I don't know. We were going into water. There at the lake, rain was so gentle. It was a drift, a veil of grey and silver, like the sails of ghost ships, gauzy. There was cloud in the rain too, white mists lifting off the lake so water tended into the air like it lived there. Slowly it stained, there was no violence to it, no individual drops, it was melting rain. The beach sunk into a deeper colour, and it happened so gradually that at first you could see no change at all. Then you would press on the sand with your toes and find it warm, slaty. The powder of it had condensed with moisture, you could squeeze it, shape it into castles and islands and towers. Whole cities we could leave moulded on the beach and all the time as we worked the rain softened them, merged into vague dream shapes, hills....

First thing in the morning, autumn's light just touching the tips of the forest, the serenity of the bay – to a city dweller – is unforgettable. Only the canoe wake betrays the stillness, and the illusion that the big trees are keeping their distance. Ashore, a heron breakfasting along the band of raupō in front of them wishes I would keep mine. Stepping into a run and flexing its wings in great downward arcs, it sweeps noisily out over the calm water.

I sensed Whanganui Inlet was an auspicious place the moment I first saw it. I keep coming back, not just on romantic, rejuvenating jaunts; more for practical advice from real nature. The inlet has given me a new awareness of the country I live in. Something has survived in its silences, something I'd been taught to believe had vanished like the huia, swept away in the vortex of colonial history. Yet in such tranquility it is impossible to ignore the message that no matter how cautiously I enter, I represent trouble. I'm the marauder, the hunter with shotgun, a lone member of the swarming species....

Spread between the tide and the trees is a diversity of life we've made a rarity – sea rushes lapped by the sea at one end, shaded palms and delicate ferns beneath them at the other, and in between, a succession of plants, each progressively less salt-tolerant. Yet, unless your gaze is led by the quirks of ecology, you might notice none of it.

Ecologists talk of such places as communities, but any sense of a co-evolved alliance between its plants is more illusory than real – another fantasy about nature, grown from our urge to divide and classify. As easily as our eyes pick out concentrations of colour and texture, we are tempted to see zones and boundaries – as if, to be able to inhabit them, the plants of places like this must organise themselves into something like societies. But the species this place attracts are no more than co-habitors, with a shared affinity for the edges of tidal inlets. What seems coordination, a special natural system to keep the sea from the trees, is revealed on close investigation to be just a collection of plants thrown together by fate and their ancient histories.

The last spring tide has left its calling cards among them: salty, white encrustations like hand-painted bands on every cylindrical rush leaf. Seen from a distance, the bands curve around the head of the inlet like a Plimsoll line. On that kind of tide I could glide the canoe right into the thick of the rushes and step out dry. Not today. Well out from the first line of shore plants, the falling neap tide maroons me in soft, cold mud. Sinking with each step, I slide the canoe toward the trees, leaving a trail infinitely less delicate than the inlet's herons and crabs. In behind the front line of rushes, twigs and logs, feathers, bones, shells and crab carapaces stranded by the tide responsible for the Plimsoll line are held up by the rushes.

This is more than just a shoreline. There seems wisdom and order in this miscellany of life at the land's edge. The big trees are only slightly above the reach of a spring tide, in 'height above sea level' terms, yet their very existence proves that the sea has not been near them for centuries. White skeletons of manuka mark the sea's most recent push inland – a spring tide, decades ago, driven in by a gale perhaps, ending yet another attempt by the forest to expand across the mudflats. Beneath the gaunt manuka trunks, the vegetation suddenly changes from rushes to salt-stunted shrubs, low and spindly at first, but rising in height with each step inland until you disappear beneath them. Many are coprosmas, almost every one, it seems, bears the large, fleshy, bright green companion leaves of mistletoe among its own tiny-leaved canopies. Underneath the shrubs, young plants seeded from the taller forest trees give you the feeling that, with half a chance, their young would overwhelm everything else were it not for the salty soil. Each autumn, hundreds of thousands of kahikatea and pukatea seeds, flicked by the wind or dropped by gravity and birds, must rain down from the big trees. Yet not one has become a seedling.

A few more steps inland, and manuka's tight, tiny leaves are replaced by a multitude of broadleaved shrubs, small trees and entanglements of kiekie and supplejack. Close to the big trees the floor is littered with jumbled masses of epiphytes that storms have thrown down from their upper reaches. The ground is also dense with kahikatea and pukatea seedlings, but none of the other big tree species. Rātā has an altogether different strategy for perpetuating its kind. Unable to establish as seeds on the forest floor, it has evolved a way of beginning life nearer the sky. Every century, as the old forest ages, rātā is increasing its presence, by germinating its seed among the epiphytes high in the kahikatea and pukatea, establishing a foothold for its vigorous vines to descend. Taking root in the fertile soil, they eventually dominate the old trees. Here in the tree-less tidal zone, the rātā has simply mimicked the strategy on low, shorter-lived shrubs. Strange, multi-trunked little rātā are now scattered through the scrub.

A bit more shoving against plants and I am looking up through lianes of kiekie to towering trunks, arcing palm fronds which reflect deep shafts of sunlight and, far above, masses of epiphytic lilies, ferns and orchids. The damp floor is a sprawling jumble of aerial roots, which rise every now and then in

great buttresses. The impression of tropical rainforest is no delusion: 30 million years ago, before the days of birds – when reptiles did the flying and seed dispersal – before the land that has become New Zealand broke away from the rest of the ancient Gondwana continent, it was mainly low-lying like this, forested and tropical. Almost every plant here, and its interaction with others derives from these tropical rainforest beginnings.

'Primeval' was how Whanganui Inlet was first described to me. Embellished no doubt by the other name in this stretch of country, Te Tai Tapu – the sacred, or as some locals prefer forbidden, coast – the image I created in my mind's eye was of a timewarp, a glimpse of coastal New Zealand before people came. The stories that drew me to it also made me so cautious about its tide that I spent my first evening watching the speed with which it came in, crept up each arm of the inlet, paused, and was sucked back across the mudflats, into its channels and out to the open sea. Next morning, to avoid a stranding, I timed my exploration around the brief hour the inlet was other than a swathe of mud. My reward was to encounter its bay of big trees from the water.

As I floated motionless, surrounded by forest, Whanganui indeed seemed one of those 'safe and commodious harbours' the first Europeans were so keen to find. The bark of a farm dog, cutting through the silence from paddocks miles away on the other side of The Entrance, brought me back to the present. North, beyond Pah Point, the Pakawau Hills lay in blue haze. West, across the emerald calm of the inlet, were the limestone bluffs from whose summits you can see down the West Coast in fine weather. East, different country altogether: low granite hills of beech forest, tried for farms but left in burnt stumps. South, the illusion of fertile plains that is in reality the largely unfarmable scrub and flax-covered peat of

Maungarakau Swamp where the inlet used to go to the sea many thousands of years ago. Then, with merely a different ripple, and a flick of the eelgrass under the canoe, the tide turned. Imperceptibly at first, forest began drifting past and I felt the pull toward the swells of the Tasman Sea.

Neck-twisting at the inlet scenery one evening, too close to The Entrance, an ebbing tide did catch me. It was clearly impossible to reach the spot where I'd left the van, so I took the next best option. An hour bent against the flow left me stranded in water too shallow for paddling, and still moving in the opposite direction. Knowing time wasn't on my side, I ran with the canoe until the film of water was too thin to slide it any more. Alternately pushing and dragging, I made it to the nearest landing, the gravel beach of Coal Point, a headland that guards the little bay of trees like a crab's pincer.

Weary from the effort, I sat down and gazed back at my tracks. The last of the sun sparkled off old bottles poking out of the mud, sand-blasted by a century's storms. Two rusted bits of a horse-drawn plough littered the beach. All around them were water-worn jet-black pebbles of coal. Offshore in the mud, I could see the last remains of the jetty from which they were spilt. A primeval place?...

Reading the landscape – like using a tiny net in a big river – you can catch only some of the infinite detail. The rest is washed away beyond memory and possession. Unequivocal facts are elusive. As Whanganui Inlet becomes a place where respect for nature means withdrawal, it becomes a place of contested values. It attracts my senses with its primeval, land-before-people meeting of forest and water – yet amiably unhidden, as though last century was yesterday, is the abundant sign of its human history.

Nevertheless, you wouldn't see an environment like this in Europe. Even in New Zealand, for such a large tidal inlet to have sneaked through the 19th and 20th centuries completely un-urbanised is an aberration. That's why so much of Te Whanganui has been designated a marine reserve. Assuming some moral duty to minimise human presence, the government that has more often got behind the campaign against nature has brought logging to a standstill and reserved the last forests, and is now doing the same to the inlet itself. That has upset those who had grown used to 'backblocks' subsidies like the 1930s Depression labour that carved the Dry Road around the inlet, and used to 'the Haven' as their unfettered domain, who have known it as a place whose hills have smouldered in the search for gold and coal and the creation of pasture – or, as the urge took someone once, just to rid the place of wasps. They know well of the endless succession of flax, timber and cattle that has gone down the inlet to sailing barques, scows and steamers. Now they are being told this is one of New Zealand's very few estuaries still in its natural state. Soon after the talk about the marine reserve started, they put a sign up beside the Dry Road:

> WESTHAVEN HUMAN RESERVE
> NO
> BIRDS, D.O.C. OR BIRD BRAINS

They are being overtaken by the growing passion for nature that is drawing more and more urbanites like me to seek the last traces of the original land. With nature now more novelty than nuisance, an out-of-the-way territory for quiet exploitation has become sudden wilderness. Curiosities in its primeval shadow, the tramway rotting into the mudflats and the shell heaps of the vanished people who called it a sacred coast, seem less important to those grappling with the prospect of a sustainable future than the notion of an unpolluted, native estuary....

It's ornamental where it's been
self-sown across the hogback,

obsequious and buttery,
cocking a snook at scars,

yellowing our quaint history
of occupation and reprise.

The spiny tangential crotch,
gullied and decorative,

I love from a distance,
a panorama over water

from lakeside to peninsula
where it's delicate in hollows,

or a topiary under heavens
cropped by the south wind.

I offer this crown of thorns
for the pity of my countrymen

unconvinced of the beauty
of their reluctant emblem: this

burnt, hacked, blitzed
exotic.

LAURIS EDMOND ◆ *September*

The mountain leaps, and stands
breaking horizons. It is the first
land out of falling waters, the wind

finds it like a discovering dove.
In the wheeling light it is still,
construing containment, poise
from the inchoate idiom of the earth.

No flower was white before this
blossoming of snow, no September
sharp with spring until this morning.
I shall learn the lessons of God
from the mountain; it has entered
my imagination: eternal indifference,
eternal scope, eternal reprieve.

The small hours. A moon-rayed closet full of dead air and burnt coal. A swaying circular motion that set my stomach floating as though on oil. As I put my feet on the floor they knocked over a cup of cold tea. It was another kind thought of the man sleeping above my head. He must have bought it at Frankton or Taumarunui and left it by my bed in case I should wake. I thanked him; and paddled to the window to see where I was. No difficulty. Close at hand Mount Ruapehu was shining in the moonlight.

I have always looked at scenery in an eighteenth-century way – a Johnsonian way that is, not Wordsworthian. It is the grandeur of man that moves me, not mountains. Mystical experience for me is not set in motion as for that good gray man of the Lakes. And so when he says:

> I have felt
> A presence that disturbs me with the joy
> Of elevated thoughts, a sense sublime
> Of something far more deeply interfused,
> Whose dwelling is the light of setting suns,
> And the round ocean and the living air,
> And the blue sky, and in the mind of man–

I say, Yes, and give my intellectual assent to his catalogue, but am moved to joy only by its last item.

The flanks of the mountain were certainly beautiful. They were smooth and pale, like cold butter. I enjoyed their slow turn about the train. No stirring in my soul, to be sure, but a calm enjoyment of beauty. I have been accused of lack of enthusiasm. A cold intellectual fish. But it's not so. I've seen a good deal of 'pure' response in my time, and seen what it leads to – fanaticism, self-indulgence, locked iron doors in the mind. I prefer the scalpel and microscope; and so have been accused of choosing them. It may have been true at one time, but not any longer. Dissect, experiment, by all means. But sooner or later one comes to the dark or Light. And entry cannot be made until the laboratory smock has been put off.

But my children have accused me of coldness, of pedantry. Even Oliver. Astonishing. A mountain to him is something to mine; a tree to mill for timber; a stream to dam. He's the cleverest of my sons, and the most limited. Full of sharp little thoughts that scurry about, pricking here, pricking there; but none escape from the box of his prejudices. His mind, it seems to me, is like an ant nest under glass. The little creatures are so busy, so full of purpose and hive-importance; they're never aware of the eye looking in. Well, Oliver; he is what he is; and he has, as they say, climbed to the top of the heap. Many people have told me I should be proud of him.

The train turned away from the mountain. I struggled into my blankets....

I invite you to join me in a voyage into the past, to that territory of the heart we call childhood. Consider, if you will, Te Parenga. A beach, three-quarters of a mile long, a hundred yards wide at low water. Rocks at either end: on the east, chunky and rounded, a squat promontory. The 'king' and 'queen' stand a few yards out from the shore: two squashed rock pillars with steps cut into their sides for diving in the summer. At high water, the sea will cover more than half of them. The rocks on the west are shallow, spreading into a terraced reef, shelving far out to sea. Here there is no smoothness. The surface of these rock shelves is jagged, cutting and tearing at the bare foot, fretted away by the corrosive sea. The receding tide leaves deep pools here where sea anemones with fronts of red and black jelly wave coloured strings to entice the shrimps, and sometimes a lone starfish lies marooned, diminishing in the sun. Ahead, across a narrow channel, central to vision and imagination, Rangitoto, enormous, majestic, spread-eagled on the skyline like a sleeping whale, declining from a central cone to the water in two huge flanges, meeting the sea in a haze of blue and green. It guards Te Parenga from wind and tempest: it has a brooding splendour.

The beach is fringed with pohutukawa trees, single and stunted in the gardens, spreading and noble on the cliffs, and in the empty spaces by the foreshore. Tiny red coronets prick through the grey-green leaves. Bark, flower and leaf seem overlaid by smoke. The red is of a dying fire at dusk, the green faded and drab. Pain and age are in these gnarled forms, in bare roots, clutching at the earth, knotting on the cliff-face, in tortured branches, dark against the washed sky.

Besides this majesty, the houses of Te Parenga have a skimped look. A low ridge curls upwards from the beach, flattening to accept the concrete ribbon of the main road north, an intermittent rash of shops on its margins, then the ridge rolls on and down to the mud-flats and mangroves of the upper harbour. The houses of Te Parenga face the sea, unlovely bungalows of wood and tin, painted red and brown to thwart the rodent air. At the end of the beach, before the main road north leaves it for ever a clot of buildings: shops, banks, the Council Chambers, the Anglican Church in wooden Gothic, cheek by jowl with the cinema – built to last – in brick.

It's only a hundred years since men dressed as chimneys, in top hats and black stove-pipes, women dressed as great bells, tiny feet as clappers, stepped ashore at Te Parenga from a broad-bellied, wind-billowed ship. They brought with them grain and root, tilling and harvest; timber trees, fruit trees, flowers, shrubs, grass; sheep, cows, horses, deer, pigs, rabbits, fish, bees; language, law, custom, clocks and coinage; Queen Victoria and her views on Heaven and Earth; The Trinity; Santa Claus and the imagery of snow where no snow will ever fall at Christmas; a thousand years of history, a shoal of shibboleths, taboos and prohibitions and the memory of a six-months' voyage. They threw them all together in a heap and stepped ashore to slash the bush, banish the natives and pray silently far into the night. They left some of the pohutukawas, and Rangitoto was beyond their reach.

This is Te Parenga: my heritage, my world....

Photo: John McDermott

123

KERI HULME ◆ from *Slipping Away from the Gaze of the Past*

an extract from *Homeplaces: Three Coasts of the South Island of New Zealand*

Moeraki, *is* —
Moeraki means, Place to Sleep (or Dream) by Day.
Moeraki was a complex of kaika and pa, and Moeraki is a
fishing port.
Moeraki is beaches and reefs, islands and volcanic dykes.
Moeraki is a motley collection of permanent homes and holi-
day baches (or cribs, as Southern idiom has it), and Moeraki is
an unmanned lighthouse, and manicured rolling-hill farms.
Moeraki is its sealife, and all its ghosts at night (indeed, it is
the only place I know of where you can meet ghosts by day).
Above all, Moeraki is people, from the remains in the ancient
habitations and urupa and middens, to the lively family cribs.

Seaweed floats in a brown tangled rack, a
tack out from the rocks.
It falls and rises, breathing with the water.

On the beach, the apricot and gold gravel
turns rusty-orange at wave-edge.
There is a long streak of iron-dark sand
where Matuatiki runs out to sea.
There are shattered black rocks round all
the arc of bay.

The cliffs are made of claystone, greenish
and ochre, with odd intrusions of pink
melted rocks. The thornbushes along the tops
slant away from the sea. They are shaved
trimmed and wounded by the wind.

At the end of the kaik' bay the cliff goes
down in humps to stand blunt-nosed
against the sea. But the rocks creep
further out, become jetty arms, reefs enclosing.
They are full of secret pools —
the unblinking eyes of octopi
at night.

Today, a cloud of midges weaves and
dances through the evening sun.
There are mysterious glassy tracks
on the sea.
Thin waves hush in, pause: slide away.
Moeraki, calm as untroubled sleep

(from *Pa Mai Tou Reo Aroha*)

I have, one way or another, been here all my life. I am not
often here, in the physical sense of occupying Moeraki-space
and Moeraki-time, but I never leave it. It sometimes seems that
I am swept by two tides, one the here & now which is the
inexorable, bringing me to death, and the other a wave burgeoning forever out of the past, bearing me aloft and away
from any future shore. Fish, water-traveller, that's me, bemused

by what-ifs and why-was-that so? and never sure of anything... o, but also the eminently practical, pragmatic Pig, islander and coastdweller, firmly rooted in earth.

An August evening, late winter, and I've come over the hill to here, to pick kareko. The fronds are at their longest now.

For quite a while, my uncle Bill lived at the kaik' beach, and any arrival was welcomed by him. Then, the cribs were warmed and ready for us, and we didn't so much settle in as shrug off one way of life and speed into another, more vivid more real than everyday. Now that Bill has retired back to the family home in Oamaru, there is cold welcome: it is a matter of unlocking doors and windows, and sweeping out dead mice and flies, and setting fires, warming the places to life again. The cribs are right on the shore, and spring tides lap over the fences, or wash up the boatramps inside. At first, they are always damp.

I do the unlocking and sweeping and lighting part as quickly as possible, and then go for a wander round the beaches.

Tena koe, e te wahi humarire, e te wahi miharo, tena koe. It's been quite a while eh? I haven't seen you since March, and I've changed a lot since then.

I can always be seduced by a tideline, any beach in the world, but Moeraki tidelines are magical. It's partly because we know them so well, and can recognise and name every kind of shell and seaweed, and wrecked bird or crab or piece of debris, but it's also because they are ever full of surprises. We never quite know what will be there, one tide to the next. Over the years, we have found broken adzes, whole pendants, and a snakeskin cowrie (did someone drop that?); a skull; dead seals, and live sealions; two bottles with unreadable messages inside, and a half-full bottle of rum; part of a weather balloon, and fragments of a boat; prints from someone who walked by early

in skindiver's flippers, and the marks of two energetic bodies and a neat pile of *seventeen* condoms — now come on, mates, what the hell were you doing? Skiting? Even if you were making balloons of them, you were pretty busy...

The tidelines stretch on, beach after beach....

Lying in a bunk in Elderslee, the oldest of the three cribs the family owns at the kaik' beach. The range fire is still going strong, and the room is full of flicker-light. Our bunks are not high, and they give a feeling of comfortable security — your own special womb-room, connected with the living space but apart from it. I imagine that a cupboard bed in an Orkney croft would be similar.

The kettles are singing over the fire: a gull keens out on the northern reef. There's a southerly blow building outside. Before I fall asleep, there is a little wittering of hail on the roof, a here & gone gust. Tomorrow will be a bleak and cold Otago day....

They say that the hole in the sea off Rerenga-wairua is fringed with kelp.

As children, we made skiddy slippers from the rimurapa fronds, and balls, that bounced, from its stipes. There are six of us today, four female and two male, and I am the oldest. We were more than a handful for my mother to bring up (for she was widowed at 31, when her youngest baby was a year old), but she didn't just cope: she enabled us to flourish, each in our own, very different ways. Some people are appalling failures as parents, and some never get the experience, and some, like my mother Mary, are extremely good at that most-important job....

A beach is promising territory for children to grow up in. There is outside room, a freedom of space, and a sufficiency of change. If you have normal skills, it is a good place to begin to learn life. You learn it from the essential fecundity, and adaptability, of sea interacting with land. You learn it from the omnipresent fact of death — bubu eats seaweed, gull eats bubu, cat gets gull. The crabs and the poti pick the bones. And, if it is a beach like the kaik' beach, you learn life from the past. It can be, in the most real and physical sense, in front of you.

For instance, you early get to know there are layers — strata of names and events that affect one another, interweavings of people from all round the planet. Nobody can give more than the proximate date for the arrival of the first humans here, but you can bet your bottom dollar they were Polynesian. They didn't call themselves 'Maori', but 'the gathering, or company of so-and-so', or 'the family of so-and-so', Te Kahui te mea-te mea, Kati Te mea-te mea. The names of some of the earliest explorers and settlers are lost in that past glowing in front of us, but Kati Mamoe (the descendants of Hotu Mamoe) retain memories that reach over 500 years. And I have inherited from my people, the family of Tahu-potiki who battled with Kati Mamoe, certainly, but who also interwed with them, I have inherited knowledge not only of *who* journeyed here, and who lived here, and how they lived and loved and hated, but also what they called the hills and reefs and beaches round.

Layers... round at the southern end of Tutakahikura beach (two bays south from the kaik'), is a headland now known as 'Te-upoko-a-Matiaha' (Mathias' Head), Matiaha being the famous Matiaha Tiramorehu, who led his people to Moeraki from Kaiapoi, and who is commemorated in the first stained-glass window depicting a Maori (in the little church Kotahitanga at Moeraki Port). When Maori-English was going strong, the point was called, 'Te *Heti* a Matiahi', but before that it was 'Te-upoko-a-Paitu', Paitu being an earlier chief. And doubtless, Waitaha and Te Kahui a Rapuwai, being earlier settlers still, had other names for it.

All this fuss over one, not large headland? Well, it *is* at the end of a dramatic beach (of which, much more, later), and behind it *is* an ancient graveyard, Uhimataitai, but the fact is that *every* headland, and rock, and islet, and hill, was named, and sometimes named many times. On the other hand, there were names that stuck, right from the beginning.

Head north, round the beaches: past the rocks of the reef Te Karipi, where I pick most of my kareko; past the island Maukiekie, and the group known as Paeko; past the bluff at Punatoetoe, and on to Onekakara the odiferous beach (and since whales were once tried out there, you can imagine 'odiferous' as a bit of an understatement). Go on, still heading north, round by Millers Bay, which was once called Karere-kautuku and which sometimes has amazing drifts and heaps of live tuatua on it. The first you know that the sea has made a gift of these succulent shellfish is the screaming of gulls. There is never enough food to stop gulls from squabbling over it... past Millers Bay, and by now you have left behind the unique gold & ochre gravel, and are travelling over dark rocks and a strange pallid sand that is streaked with something like oil. It is a broad beach you are on, with a correspondingly wide sweep of bay.

The great canoe *Te Araiteuru* had made the voyage from the central Pacific without coming to grief. She had stopped at Turanga, where kumara were planted (and that planting place is to this day called Araiteuru), and journeyed south to Kaikoura, where more kumara were established. Then, still with a substantial cargo aboard — kumara, and gourds, taro and foodbaskets — she came sweeping downwind to the Otakou coast.

What happened then is uncertain: there is an old waiata, song-poem, that says she broached, and was overwhelmed by three gigantic waves — Otewao, Otoko, and Okaka were *their* names — having earlier had the misfortune to lose her bailer. (I have been told by other elders that this waiata applies to a much later, but equally sacred and renowned vessel, the ancestral waka *Takitimu*.) Whatever, after that long and useful journey, she wrecked, and is commemorated by the reef called after her.

And she is remembered by something else: here, on the beach with pallid sand, is her cargo.

Mention the name 'Moeraki' to most New Zealanders, and you will be rewarded with a blank stare, or a bright smile and, 'O yes! That's where the boulders are!'

Well, not quite.

But the boulders deserve their reputation. There is nothing quite like them almost anywhere else in the world. The largest is well over six feet in diameter, a septarian concretion with yellow calcite crystals at its core. There are dozens of them (there used to be hundreds, but all of the accessible smaller ones have been souvenired), round and weird, and looming on the bare curving beach.

You think six-feet plus is a bit big for a food basket or a gourd?

Araiteuru was not your average waka: her crew was distinctly strange — many of them turned into hills and rocks in the near vicinity, for example — and so why should her cargo be of an inferior nature? As I grew, I may have begun to doubt the literal truth of the story of *Araiteuru*, but do I remember which canoe brought the kumara, and who came with it?

Forever.

As children, we went mainly to the boulders for mussels, or to play in the sinking sand round their bases. That was a thrill: the pale sand seemed to have no bottom and sucked you in, to your thighs, with surprising ease and swiftness. None of us were ever game to let go and see how deep you could sink. We held grimly onto a crack or a ledge of the boulder (they may take up to four million years to form, but they erode quickly: I have watched two vanish in my forty-odd years) and sort of enjoyed the sensation. A lot of screaming went on.

The mussels, those stubby fat blueblack southern kutae, have eroded away entirely over the years, from the scouring of the sand, and the overpicking by humans.

Things change: things erode: things go.

The shoreward rocks of Tikoraki, the reef that protects the south end of the kaik' bay, are being cracked and hammered apart.

'Shoulda put concrete on them years ago, when we had the chance', grumbles my uncle Bill Miller. He means, he should have done it when he was younger and had the strength. He knows I won't do it: I'm a believer in the dance of change. The sea gives, and the sea takes away, and if it breaks up Tikoraki and devastates the cribs, even the beloved Black Bach that I look after — and it is most likely to take that crib first, because it is southernmost on the beach — well, so be it.

I know this place as well as I know my own body, and better than I know my own mind. It is where I've done most of my growing up. It is where I'd prefer to be buried, here among ancestral bones. I love it better than any place on Earth. It is my turangawaewae-ngakau, the standing-place of my heart, and I expect, and receive, strength and energy and love from it.

But I never expect it to stay exactly the same. None of my homeplaces do that.

That old grey rogue the sealman
has come ashore at last
hollow-flanked and flippers folded
over the curl of his breast
he can still yawn, pink gape and yellowed, warning, teeth—
and rub hinder webs slowly together
as though he really waits upon
the benefice of sun...

My mother Mary and uncle Bill have come for the weekend, so I've shifted out of Elderslee and along to the Black Bach. It's the crib I'm kaitiaki for, guardian of & caretaker to: Bill and his mate Tui McNeil built it over 40 years ago, before I was born. They coated the walls with tar then, to prevent rot and protect it against the sea, and it has stayed tar-coated ever since. The walls are not quite the same ones Bill and Tui erected. In 1975, there was a king tide, that dangerous combination of extraordinarily high spring-tide and onshore wind. Waves were breaking over the roof of the black crib before the tide's end, smashing in the doors and filling the living-room and the boatshed with sand. Other cribs fared worse: two were wrecked entirely, and have never been rebuilt. Bill remade the doors, and reskinned the walls, up to four thicknesses of plywood and corrugated iron, after we had spent a merry week digging all three cribs out. I understand there is another king tide due at the end of this year. This time, it will be my turn to lie on my belly on the cliff above the Black Bach and wonder how anything humanly built can survive the power of the sea.

Meantime, I've lit the musterer's stove (a little cast-iron affair a foot by eighteen inches by a foot deep), and got rid of the latest crop of dead things. The tide is coming in, and it's getting dark. On the horizon beyond Tikoraki, a hunter's moon is rising, hugely inflated looking, smokey-orange in colour. I'll get the lamps going soon, and do some reading, then go to bed with the doors wide open and fall asleep listening to the soft swash of quiet waves curling up the boat-ramp and over the doorstep.

It's nearly the end of August, and time to be going home. Slim and Rose Dalton up the hill will keep an eye on this crib until they see I've taken the window shutter down, and have my windfish flying on a bamboo pole outside, to show I'm home here, again....

M K JOSEPH ◆ *Distilled Water*

From Blenheim's clocktower a cheerful bell bangs out
The hour, and time hangs humming in the wind.
Time and the honoured dead. What else? The odd
Remote and shabby peace of a provincial town.
Blenkinsopp's gun? the Wairau massacre?
Squabbles in a remote part of empire.
Some history. Some history, but not much.

Consider now the nature of distilled
Water which has boiled and left behind
In the retort rewarding sediment
Of salts and toxins. Chemically pure of course
(No foreign bodies here) but to the taste
Tasteless and flat. Let it spill on the ground,
Leach out its salts, accumulate its algae,
Be living: the savour's in impurity.
Is that what we are? something that boiled away
In the steaming flask of nineteenth-century Europe?
Innocuous until now, or just beginning
To make its own impression on the tongue.

And through the Tory Channel naked hills
Gully and slip pass by, monotonously dramatic
Like bad blank verse, till one cries out for
Enjambement, equivalence, modulation,
The studied accent of the human voice,
Or the passage opening through the windy headlands
Where the snowed Kaikouras hang in the air like mirage
And the nation of gulls assembles on the waters
Of the salt sea that walks about the world.

BRIAN TURNER ◆ *Visiting Kai Kai Beach*

(for Barbara and Ngaire and Erik)

We came this way once and would hope
to come again, by land or sea,

in whichever season the weather
or physics of the body allows, for that,

finally, is what it amounts to. From the
steepening slopes of the hill above the bay

we disturbed a flock of geese
and a few young Herefords, and picked

our way among a rash of bloated dead sheep.
Below, red-brown rushes sat like shaving brushes

beside the brackish creek which petered out
behind low dunes and a flat sandy beach.

The sou'wester blustered but didn't bother us
and the sun's light smarted

on the shivering reaches of Blueskin Bay.
We climbed the tow-browed cliffs

at the southern end of the beach
and wandered along the gently-sloping headland

to the light on Heywards Point. There, we lay
in ripe grass in the warm late winter sun

and felt the ancients move among surrounding hills,
felt the pulse and poise of time,

and watched and listened as the sea birds
hovered above the cliff's edge. It seemed

as if antiquity descended upon us.
We listened to the suck and lall of the sea

and one white sail beat towards us
across the blistering broad bay.

CHARLIE DOUGLAS ◆ from *Mr Explorer Douglas*

Karangaroa [Karangarua] River
8 June 1892

J. Strauchon Esq., C.S.

Sir,

I have the honor now to write out full particulars of my trip up Copeland [Copland] and Karangaroa River. If I have failed in the main object, to discover a pass available for Mule traffic to the Hermitage, the Survey will now have the block filled in for good, and Adventurous Tourists who cross the range will at least know what they have to contend with before reaching the Coast....

The first 3 miles up the Copland is tolerable travelling. The river rises in that distance some 300 feet with high flat terraces on either side most of the way up, but 20 chains above Architect Creek, the gorge commences and the river rises 1200 feet in 2 $\frac{1}{2}$ miles. This is not a true gorge, as in no case do the cliffs approach nearer than ten chains. Perhaps the best description of it is a natural sluice box very badly paved. On the North side, there is a well defined terrace some 300 feet above the river bed, running up to the Flats. This terrace is rolled wash, with morainic drift dumped on the top, but on the south side from the cliffs to the river bed the hill sides are covered with immense boulders tumbled and tossed about in chaotic confusion. The occasional glimpses a traveller gets of the river while peeping through between or under boulders like small hills is in my opinion the best scene on the Copeland for beauty. The river cataracts come rushing out of the most unlikely places, and over rocks worn into fantastic shapes by the action of the water, away thirty and forty feet up, snags and

fragment of trees perched on rocks or caught fast in trees show the height of the river in floods. Some idea of the size of the boulders can be formed by one I measured, it is a mass of rock fallen from above and stands on a ledge five hundred up and away from the River. It is a flat square 300 feet of a side - 1200 in circumference and 120 high with large Rata trees growing on the top.

Those trees, like most which grow on such boulders, in course of time find a want of either water or soil, so nature has ingeniously supplied the want by causing the trees to send roots down the face of the Rock to the ground below. A little above this boulder but in the river bed is another curiosity, "The Chair"; it is a large rock hollowed and shaped like a chair, it would just fit the Statue of Memnon only he would have to tuck his legs up. The Forrest in the gorge is a mixture of cedar, Totara, Rata, Kamai and the usual underscrub. The Cedars and Totara are in many cases of immense size, but they are too much scattered to be of any market value, except for local consumption such as bridge, cribb work or snow sheds in the event of a track ever being brought down the Copeland. Totara of a certain sort is common enough in Westland, but the real article, all heart and no sap, is much scarcer than people suppose, so the presence of it in the Karangaroa and branches is worth noting....

After a weary rough scramble through the Gorge, the Flats commence. These are about two miles long and a mile broad from the foot of the hills. They are partly open river bed and partly Ribbon wood and Ake Ake scrub (one peculiarity of the bush is it has a lean up the River, showing that the winds

almost all blow up)—scrub with low grassed Terraces running parallel with the River. In ancient days it has been a glacier basin, then probably a lake which has gradually filled with gravell. Aniseed and other mountain plants show how little effect sun has on the flats. Such basins are very common up West Coast rivers. In fact every large stream has one or more of them, some well grassed and others so. So those in valleys running north and south may be of some value when population forces its way into the Mountains, but those like the Copland lying East and West are almost useless unless in a very wide valley, as for five and six months the year they are practically Sunless. Those above the 2000 feet level are some times snowed in for months. However they are a Godsend to travellers, the delight of breaking out on one of them after miles of scrambling in dense bush more than repays all the trouble, and then the Scenery can be appreciated. Occasional glimpses of Peaks and Glaciers through dense foliage may be very pretty and verry Artistic but they are aggravating to ordinary mortals.

The scenery from the Copland Flats is splendid; to the North Mt. Lyttle towers up looking far higher than it really is. The peak is a well formed Tent ridge and the slopes of the mountain are covered with a splendid Glacier of the third class. This Glacier is very steep and is continually sending down masses of snow and blocks of Ice and rocks.

In severe winter the Snow slope from Lyttle comes down to near the Flats, as shown by gravell and small rocks lying on the top of boulders in that peculiar losely packed way which only melting snow can give. When in that state the scene must be magnificent; a towering peak and a Glacier terminating in a long serpent like slope of white snow flanked by dark bush and still darker cliffs. If a road was only through this country, Winter would be the time to visit it. Not to cross the range, that would be rather dangerous, but to see what the Mountains really looks like when clothed in white (then is the time to hear the Avalanche and to learn what driving snow really means. It is not by trotting out of a comfortable hotel and back the same day that natures wonders can really be seen.) Let some enterprising Tourist or alpine explorer just try up a Westland River in the winter and the glories of the mountains will show themselves to his eyes. The extra dangers at that season are mostly imaginary, though the extra discomfort is certainly not....

Away on the south side of the flats is one of the wonders of the Copeland, namely the Sierra. The Jagged peaks and broken face of the Wakatipu "Remarkables", all that I have read or seen of rugged ridges or mountain, sink into insignificance before this wonderfull sight. A range of broken shattered cliffs, topped by a serrated ridge looking as if some Giant with little skill and a very bad file had attempted to make a saw out of the Mountains. "The Splinter" is an immense slab of rock pointing along the ridge, but its end standing out from the solid hundreds of feet; other points and slabs look as if the slightest shock would send them tumbling into space. Wherever a glimpse can be obtained of the slope to the southward, masses of snow show the presence of a large snowfield over the ridge. The whole ridge is unmistakable evidence that no Earthquake of a severe character has shaken this part of the Island for ages, as such a shock would have brought most of the jagged tops down to the foot of the cliffs. The sketch sent with the map gives a very poor idea of this ridge, but no doubt it is better than no Sketch and will at least give some idea of what I have faintly attempted to discribe. Other countries may show better Glaciers, higher mountains, than the Copeland but I doubt if anything like the Sierra can be seen away from the Moon as seen through a large Telescope....

The River all the way up to and near the Glacier is

unfordable and unjumpable and up the Marchant for two miles it is the same, so as we were on the wrong side of the river and had to go up to Baker's Saddle somehow, it became a question of throwing a spar accross, but here was the difficulty. A good place to cross had no spar handy, and vice-a-versa. At last near the middle Forks we found a large flat rock standing in the middle of the river and away 300 feet up the hill was a Cedar spar about fifty feet long. This we cut and lowered with the rope and after some manoeuvering it was proped up against the rock at a considerable angle. I scrambled up hauled up the swags, and the next thing was to get Betsey across. The spar was too step for her to walk, so we made her fast to the middle of the rope and it was haul away, and I'll never forget the imploring look and howl of that valuable animal as she felt herself launched into space over a foaming torrent. The other end of the rock was a short spring into shallow water. The swags were launched over, the Dog prefered to to jump, and the Copeland was crossed in safety.

(In order to retain authenticity, the original spellings have been reproduced.)

ACKNOWLEDGEMENTS

The publishers gratefully acknowledge permission to reproduce copyright passages from the following copyright holders and publishers:

James K Baxter, from *Collected Poems of James K Baxter* (Oxford University Press Australia and New Zealand 1980 and Mrs J Baxter, ©The Estate of James K Baxter); Charles Brasch, *Indirections* (Oxford University Press 1980); Alistair Te Ariki Campbell, from *Pocket Collected Poems* (Hazard Press 1996); Allen Curnow, from *Early Days Yet: New & Collected Poems 1991-1997* (Auckland University Press 1997); Ruth Dallas, from *Collected Poems* (University of Otago Press 1987); Charlie Douglas (Ed. John Pascoe), *Mr Explorer Douglas* (AH & AW Reed 1957); Basil Dowling, from *Canterbury and Other Poems* (Caxton Press, 1949); Lauris Edmond, from *Selected Poems 1975-1994* (Bridget Williams Books, 1994); A R D Fairburn, *The Estuary* (A R D Fairburn Literary Estate); Fiona Farrell, *A Story About Skinny Louie* (Penguin Books (NZ) Ltd); Janet Frame, from *Living in the Maniototo* (published in Great Britain by the Women's Press Ltd, 1981, 34 Great Sutton Street, London EC1V OLQ, used by permission of The Women's Press Ltd and Curtis Brown (Aust) Pty Ltd, Sydney); Maurice Gee, *Plumb* (Oxford University Press, 1979 and Richards Literary Agency); Denis Glover, from *Come High Water* (Dunmore Press 1977 and The Granville Glover Family Trust); Kirsty Gunn, *Rain* (Faber and Faber); Patricia Grace, *Waiariki* (Penguin Books (NZ) Ltd, 1986); Keri Hulme (with photographs by Robin Morrison), *Homeplaces: Three Coasts of the South Island of New Zealand* (Hodder & Stoughton 1989); Sam Hunt, from *Collected Poems* (Penguin Books (NZ) Ltd, 1980); Kapka Kassabova, *Reconnaissance* (Penguin Books (NZ) Ltd, 1999); Witi Ihimaera, *Tangi* (Auckland, 1972 with permission from Reed Publishing (NZ) Ltd); M K Joseph, *Distilled Water* (Estate of M K Joseph); Elizabeth Knox, *When We Stopped* (Sport 15, 1995); John A Lee, *Delinquent Days* (Collins, 1967); Owen Marshall, from *Timeless Land* (Longacre Press, 1996); Bruce Mason, *The End Of The Golden Weather* (Victoria University Press, 1981); Ronald Hugh Morrieson, *Came A Hot Friday* (Penguin Books (NZ) Ltd, 1982); John Mulgan, *Man Alone* (Longman Paul 1972/Penguin 1990); Chris Orsman, *Ornamental Gorse* (Victoria University Press, 1994); Geoff Park, *Nga Uruora - The Groves Of Life* (Victoria University Press, 1995); C K Stead, from *Straw Into Gold* (Auckland University Press, 1997); Frank Sargeson, *Once Is Enough* (A H & A W Reed, 1973, and The Sargeson Trust); Maurice Shadbolt, *A Touch Of Clay* (David Ling, 1983); H Guthrie Smith, *Tutira: The Story of a New Zealand Sheep Station* (AH & AW Reed, 1969); Brian Turner, from *Listening To The River* (John McIndoe 1983); Hone Tuwhare, from *Shape Shifter* (Steele Roberts, 1997) and *Deep River Talk* (Godwit Publishing, 1993); Aat Vervoorn, *Beyond the Snowline* (AH & AW Reed/John McIndoe 1981); Ian Wedde, *Symmes Hole* (Penguin Books (NZ) Ltd, 1986) and from *The Shirt Factory and Other Stories* (Victoria University Press, 1981).

All efforts have been made to contact the correct copyright holders. The publishers would appreciate being contacted directly to put right any omissions or mistakes.

CAPTIONS

Photographic Note – A number of the photographs selected for this book have not been taken in the exact location described by the author. This is either because we have been unable to find an image that does justice to the relevant poem or prose extract, or because the landscape exists only in the author's imagination. In both cases however, we have tried to find a photograph that, while not geographically accurate, captures something of the spirit of the landscape evoked in the writing.

Page 6 -   Near Ward, Marlborough
Page 23 -   Podocarp forest, Westland National Park
Page 25 -   Kanuka trees north of Auckland
Page 29 -   Sunrise at the head of the Tasman Glacier, Aoraki/ Mount Cook National Park
Page 31 -   Mt Bevan, Mount Aspiring National Park
Page 33 -   Franz Josef Glacier, Westland National Park
Page 35 -   Pakawau, Golden Bay
Page 38 -   Above the Huka Falls, Central North Island
Page 41 -   Near Tarras, Central Otago
Page 43 -   Hawkes Bay farmland
Page 45 -   Shelter belt, North Canterbury
Page 47 -   Near Bendigo, Central Otago
Page 49 -   Ridge above the Wahianoa River, Tongariro National Park
Page 51 -   Beech-forested gorge, Kaimanawa Ranges
Page 53 -   Whanganui River
Page 57 -   Burnt forest, Wairarapa Coast
Page 59 -   Salvation Army Citadel, Oamaru
Page 61 -   Pacific Ocean
Page 63 -   Farm gate, Waiho Valley, South Westland
Page 65 -   Outhouse, Mitimiti, Northland
Page 67 -   Collapsed swingbridge, Whanganui River
Page 71 -   Evening, Wellington harbour

Page 73 -   Mt Ngauruhoe from the east, Tongariro National Park
Page 75 -   Sunrise east of the Main Divide, Aoraki/Mount Cook National Park
Page 79 -   Mangroves, Manukau Harbour
Page 81 -   Moonrise, Golden Bay
Page 83 -   Mist forest, Little Barrier Island
Page 85 -   Sunrise, Kaikoura
Page 89 -   Shore platform near East Cape
Page 91 -   Fire on the beach, Pakawau, Golden Bay
Page 93 -   Sunset, Kapiti Island
Page 95 -   Otago Peninsula
Page 99 -   The Main Divide south of Aoraki/Mt Cook
Page 101 - Red Crater, Mt Tongariro, Tongariro National Park
Page 103 - Painted rafters, Rongopai Meeting House, Waituhi, Gisborne
Page 105 - Detail of painted rafter, Rongopai Meeting House, Waituhi, Gisborne
Page 108 - Suburbs, Dunedin
Page 111 - Rain, Lake Taupo
Page 114 - Estuary and podocarp forest, Whanganui Inlet, Northwest Nelson
Page 117 - Denniston, West Coast
Page 119 - Evening light, Mt Taranaki
Page 121 - Eastern slopes of Mt Ruapehu, Tongariro National Park
Page 123 - Cheltenham Beach and Rangitoto Island, Auckland (Photo: John McDermott)
Page 126 - Tutakahikura (The Midden Mine, Barracouta Bay), near Moeraki (Photo: Robin Morrison)
Page 131 - Seagull, Cook Strait
Page 133 - Otago Peninsula
Page 135 - Sierra Range, Copland Valley, Westland National Park (Photo: Scott Freeman)
Page 137 - Schist boulders, Dart River, Mount Aspiring National Park